Cambridge Elements

Elements in the Philosophy of Immanuel Kant
edited by
Desmond Hogan
Princeton University
Howard Williams
University of Cardiff
Allen Wood
Indiana University

KANT'S THEORY OF CONSCIENCE

Samuel Kahn
Indiana University-Purdue University, Indianapolis

CAMBRIDGE
UNIVERSITY PRESS

CAMBRIDGE
UNIVERSITY PRESS

University Printing House, Cambridge CB2 8BS, United Kingdom

One Liberty Plaza, 20th Floor, New York, NY 10006, USA

477 Williamstown Road, Port Melbourne, VIC 3207, Australia

314–321, 3rd Floor, Plot 3, Splendor Forum, Jasola District Centre, New Delhi – 110025, India

79 Anson Road, #06–04/06, Singapore 079906

Cambridge University Press is part of the University of Cambridge.

It furthers the University's mission by disseminating knowledge in the pursuit of education, learning, and research at the highest international levels of excellence.

www.cambridge.org
Information on this title: www.cambridge.org/9781108717359
DOI: 10.1017/9781108694278

First published 2021

A catalogue record for this publication is available from the British Library.

ISBN 978-1-108-71735-9 Paperback
ISSN 2397-9461 (online)
ISSN 2514-3824 (print)

Kant's Theory of Conscience

Elements in the Philosophy of Immanuel Kant

DOI:10.1017/9781108694278
First published online: April 2021

Samuel Kahn
Indiana University-Purdue University, Indianapolis
Author for correspondence: Samuel Kahn, kahnsa@iupui.edu

Abstract: The main body of this Element, about Kant's theory of conscience, is divided into two sections. The first focuses on exegesis of Kant's ethics. One of the overarching theses of this section of the Element is that, although many of Kant's claims about conscience are *prima facie* inconsistent, a close examination of context generally can dissolve apparent contradictions. The second section of the main body of this Element focuses on philosophical issues in Kantian ethics. One of the overarching theses of this section is that many positions traditionally associated with Kantian ethics, including the denial of moral luck, the nonaccidental rightness condition, and the guise of the objectively good, are at variance with Kant's ethics.

Keywords: Kant's ethics, conscience, Kantian ethics, Kant's moral psychology, moral luck

ISBNs: 9781108717359 (PB), 9781108694278 (OC)
ISSNs: 2397-9461 (online), 2514-3824 (print)

Contents

1 Introduction

Compared to other aspects of Kant's practical philosophy, Kant's theory of conscience remains relatively unexplored in the secondary literature on his work. This is no doubt due, at least in part, to the fact that in the *Groundwork of the Metaphysics of Morals* (henceforth *Groundwork*) and the *Critique of Practical Reason*, Kant's two most widely read works on ethics, conscience plays very little role.[1]

However, Kant has extended discussions of conscience in three of his lesser-read works: "On the Miscarriage of all Philosophical Attempts in Theodicy" (henceforth "Miscarriage"), *Religion within the Boundaries of Mere Reason* (henceforth *Religion*), and the *Metaphysics of Morals*. There are also many unpublished notes in which Kant discusses conscience, and it may be conjectured, on the basis of extant copies of students' notes, that conscience was a frequent topic in Kant's lectures.

As commentators have begun to pay closer attention to these lesser-read works, the literature on Kant's theory of conscience has begun to develop. It is thanks to this development that this Element is possible: there is an emerging consensus that Kant's theory of conscience is important both in its own right and insofar as it can help to correct various misunderstandings that have become part of the standard view of Kant's ethical thought.

The main body of this Element is divided into two sections. Section 2 focuses on exegesis of Kant's ethics. One of the overarching theses of this section of the Element is that, although many of Kant's claims about conscience are *prima facie* inconsistent, a close examination of context generally can dissolve apparent contradictions. Section 3 of the Element focuses on philosophical issues in Kantian ethics. One of the overarching theses of this section is that many positions traditionally associated with Kantian ethics, including the denial of moral luck, the nonaccidental rightness condition, and the guise of the objectively good, are at variance with Kant's ethics.

I would like to conclude this section with a personal note about why I thought it appropriate to dedicate this particular work to my teachers. I do not know whether this is a common experience, but in my case, my teachers have believed in me, supported me, and spurred me on to do better work notwithstanding having what, on reflection, I consider a poor evidentiary base. Indeed, that even occurred in this Element, the first draft of which was garbage: I rewrote it only because one of my

---

[1] I am able to find only three mentions of conscience in these two works, each time merely in passing: GMS, AA 04: 404.20; GMS, AA 04: 422.19; and KpV, AA 05: 098.14. Note that all references to Kant's work use the standard academy pagination. The academy pagination can usually be found in the margins of translations of these texts. I have consulted, when possible, the Guyer/Wood Cambridge Edition translations. But all translations (and errors) here are my own.

teachers believed in me enough to think I could do better. I leave it to them to determine whether their continued support of me could be in accordance with the strict standards of belief associated with a Kantian faculty of conscience. But I do hope to convey some small measure of my heartfelt gratitude.

2 Kant's Ethics

As noted in Section 1, this part of the Element is exegetical. I have divided what I take to be Kant's most important remarks on conscience into five themed subsections. In subsection 2.1, I examine Kant's definitions of conscience and the functions he attributes to it. In subsection 2.2, I examine his position on errors of conscience. In subsection 2.3, I examine Kant's ideas about acting in accordance with conscience. In subsection 2.4, I examine the ways in which Kant uses ideas about conscience to illustrate his commitment to strict evidentialism and freedom of conscience. In subsection 2.5, I examine how Kant's ideas about conscience bear on his theism.

2.1 Definitions

Conscience is, for Kant, a mental faculty, or at the very least a capacity that arises as the result of the interplay of other mental faculties. As such, I begin by delineating the functions Kant assigns to it. The most essential function of conscience, for Kant, is to determine whether an agent has acted in accordance with the moral law. In the *Metaphysics of Morals*, Kant compares conscience to a criminal court. Kant describes conscience as having a second-order function, one that subsumes the activities of other mental faculties. According to Kant, the faculty of moral understanding determines the moral rule, playing the role of moral legislator; the faculty of judgment decides whether a given action, as falling under this law, has taken place and then imputes the action to the agent; and the faculty of reason then either acquits or condemns the agent.[2] Kant says that "all of this happens before a court ... called a court of justice" and uses this to define conscience: "The consciousness of an *inner court of justice* in the human ('before which his thoughts themselves accuse or excuse one another') is **conscience**."[3] From this it may be seen that, for Kant, whereas a criminal court determines whether a criminal is innocent or guilty of a given crime, the court of conscience determines whether an agent has acted in conformity with or contrary to the moral law in a given instance.

Kant assigns a similar function to conscience in the *Religion*. In the *Religion*, Kant says that "[t]his spirit [viz., the Holy Ghost, as opposed to God the father

---

[2] MS, AA 06: 437.32–438.08. [3] MS, AA 06: 438.08–12.

or God the son] ... is at the same time the actual judge of men (through their conscience)."[4] He then distinguishes between two kinds of judging: (1) judging in regard to merit and lack of merit, and (2) judging in regard to guilt and innocence. According to Kant, God "in his son" passes judgment of the first kind, and this kind of judgment involves interpersonal comparison. The second kind of judgment, by way of contrast, is what God as the Holy Spirit is responsible for, and such a judgment is "about *one and the same* person before a court (conscience)."[5]

Kant's parsing of the trinity is unimportant for current purposes. What is important is that conscience, for Kant, is involved in judging whether an agent is worthy of reproach for having infringed on duty. To be clear, this is not to be understood as reproach in the eyes of others. Kant's idea is not that conscience judges whether others' censure is justified. Rather, conscience judges whether an agent's behavior has measured up to the strict standard of the moral law. Others might engage in blame behavior or resent someone for infringing on a duty. But blame, for Kant, is fundamentally personal; there is, for Kant, a fact of the matter, one independent of any blame-practices or interpersonal feelings or judgments, about whether an agent is blameworthy, and it is this fact that the faculty of conscience uncovers. (There also might be a fact about whether an agent deserves merit. But that is not, according to this passage, the domain of conscience.)

There are many unpublished notes in which Kant assigns a similar function to conscience.[6] For example, in a note dated to 1783–4, Kant gives a twofold definition of conscience.[7] He says that conscience is "the capacity to become conscious of the rightfulness or wrongfulness of one's own actions" and also "the inner standing of the evaluatory capacity, as that of a judge, to draw us to account regarding the permission of our actions."[8] In a note dated to 1773–8,

---

[4] RGV, AA 06: 145.29–34.   [5] RGV, AA 06: 146.19.

[6] These notes are taken from a variety of sources. They are taken from textbooks that Kant used for teaching and then scribbled marginal notes in; from copies of Kant's own works that he went through and annotated; and from loose sheets of paper, old letters and the like, on which Kant wrote down ideas and keywords. They include rough drafts of works intended for publication (including drafts of works that eventually were published, like the *Metaphysics of Morals*) in various degrees of completion; and they include the parts of the project Kant was working on during the last years of his life, published after his death sometimes as a standalone work called the *Opus Postumum*.

[7] The dating of these notes is both imprecise and of questionable accuracy. The standard dating used today (which will be used here) was set out by the Kant scholar Erich Adickes in the first half of the twentieth century. He relied on contextual clues (such as dates on letters for notes written on correspondence); changes in handwriting (both style and ink); placement of text on a page (e.g., if a note is written between the lines of another one, then it must have come later); and other clues to piece together a rough chronological map. The mapping seems to be reasonable, all things considered, but (to use an idea of Kant's own) it is doubtful whether many would wager much on it.

[8] Refl, AA 18: 579.04–07.

Kant writes that conscience is "the consciousness of the duty to be honest in the imputation of one's own deed,"[9] and he then goes on, as in the *Metaphysics of Morals*, to compare conscience to a court of law, one in which "understanding [is] the lawgiver, the power of judgment [is] the prosecutor and the advocate, but reason is the judge."[10] And a short note from 1772–8 says merely: "conscience, which reproaches and imputes."[11]

A similar lesson may also be drawn from the discussions of conscience that can be found throughout the extant sets of students' notes from Kant's lectures.[12] For example, in one set of notes, conscience is defined as "an instinct according to which our actions 1. are imputed and 2. applied to the law 3. as well as judged with rightful force. In general it is the drive in our nature to judge ourselves."[13] And then, about thirty pages later, in the same set of notes, this is repeated: conscience is claimed to be "an instinct to judge oneself morally."[14] In another set of lecture notes it is claimed that "there is thus an instinct to judge about our actions . . . and this is conscience."[15] This claim is then echoed about fifty pages later (in the same set of notes): "conscience is an instinct to judge oneself according to moral laws."[16] And in a third set of lecture notes it is claimed that conscience is "the capacity to impute to oneself one's own factum through the law."[17]

---

[9] Refl, AA 19: 170.23–24.

[10] Refl, AA 19: 170.26–27. This idea is also found in Kant's correspondence. For example, see his 1792 letter to Maria von Herbert (Br, AA 11: 333.29–33).

[11] Refl, AA 15: 149.09.

[12] There seems to have been a regular trade in these notebooks when Kant was alive, with students buying and selling them as study guides to accompany Kant's lectures. As such, it is not known either when or by whom the still surviving notebooks were written. It is not known even how many authors contributed to a single notebook. One thing that does seem apparent is that most of these texts are multiply removed from Kant: Kant gave a lecture; someone took notes during the lecture; someone extrapolated those notes into a text in prose form outside of the lecture; someone copied that text, perhaps emending, extrapolating, and interpreting as they went; someone received that text, perhaps emending again; and so on. By means of careful (and painstaking) detective work, scholars sometimes have been able to arrive at more or less reliable conjectures about the rough origins of one or another of these texts. But it is notable that even if there were verbatim transcripts of Kant's lectures, it still would be unclear to what extent the views expressed should be taken as Kant's own. For my part, I would be more than a little apprehensive if someone were to use, without warning, a lecture transcript from a day in one of my classes as the basis of a substantive interpretation of my thought.

[13] V-PP/Powalski, AA 27: 162.04–07.   [14] V-PP/Powalski, AA 27: 196.16–17.

[15] V-Mo/Collins, AA 27: 297.05–06.   [16] V-Mo/Collins, AA 27: 351.22–23.

[17] V-MS/Vigil, AA 27: 575.27–28. Often when it is claimed that conscience is an instinct, it is also claimed that conscience is not a capacity. This distinction is not always explained. But at least once it is said to consist in the fact that an instinct is not under voluntary control: the text argues that, although agents do have the capacity to judge their own actions voluntarily, conscience does so regardless of agents' wills (V-Mo/Collins, AA 27: 351.22–30).

However, the inconsistency between the passages in which the texts claim that conscience is not a capacity and the ones in which the texts claim that it is a capacity might be merely verbal.

The function of judging whether an agent is guilty of an obligation infringement is linked up to a second function that Kant assigns to conscience: causing pain. As evidence for this, consider the following passage from Kant's *Metaphysics of Morals*:

> The pain which a person would feel from the bites of conscience, although its origin is moral, is nevertheless physical according to its effect, just as peevishness, fear, and every other morbid condition.[18]

According to Kant, pain is the effect of the reproaches (bites) of conscience that an agent feels when s/he fails to fulfill prescriptions (or proscriptions) of the moral law.

A few pages later in the *Metaphysics of Morals*, Kant remarks that conscience is one of several "*aesthetic* and preceding but natural predispositions of the mind (*praedispositio*) to be affected by concepts of duty."[19] Kant's idea in this passage is that without conscience (and these other predispositions), a being could not be moral to begin with. Kant's wording has suggested to some commentators that conscience, in addition to whatever other roles it may play in Kant's moral psychology, is itself a feeling.[20] Indeed, in the Cambridge Edition of the Works of Immanuel Kant, the word I have translated as "aesthetic" (*ästhetisch*) and which appears also in the title of the section is translated in both places as "feeling." In my view, this interpretation is not well supported by the text. Kant does not explicitly say that conscience is a feeling. But he does explicitly say, in the passage just above, that conscience causes feeling. And he also says explicitly in this passage that conscience is "not of empirical origin" and that conscience has the power "to *affect* the moral feeling through its act."[21] Moreover, in the passage from which the court metaphor that opened this subsection is taken, Kant says conscience is an "intellectual ... predisposition."[22] These claims are in tension with the idea that conscience is itself a feeling. Based on this (i.e., the lack of explicit support and the tension it

---

For example, only about forty pages after the claim that conscience is the capacity of imputation in the passage to which this note is appended, conscience is compared to apperceptio:

> Conscientia taken generally is the consciousness of oneself like apperceptio; in specie it involves the consciousness of my will, my disposition, / to do right, or that the action is right, = hence a consciousness of that which for itself is duty.
>
> (V-MS/Vigil, AA 27: 613.38–614.03)

The reason this would render the inconsistency merely verbal is that apperceptio, as used here, is not a faculty that is under voluntary control. This suggests that the word "capacity" is not used univocally in these seemingly inconsistent passages.

[18] MS, AA 06: 394.03–05.   [19] MS, AA 06: 399.10–12.
[20] Wood (2008, chapter 10, section 1).
[21] MS, AA 06: 399.14–15 and 400.30, emphasis mine.   [22] MS, AA 06: 438.24–25.

would create with Kant's other claims about conscience), I suggest that the interpretation of conscience as a feeling is mistaken.[23] I suggest, further, that Kant's claims about conscience being an aesthetic predisposition might be related to the claim, seen earlier in the lecture notes, that conscience is an instinct. The key here is that conscience is not entirely under voluntary control, something I shall return to momentarily.

Kant draws attention to an asymmetry in the feelings caused by conscience. Although Kant thinks that conscience can cause an agent pain (by means of reproaches and "bites of conscience"), he does not think that conscience can cause an agent to feel positive joy: "bliss in the comforting encouragement of one's conscience is not *positive* (as joy) but rather only *negative* (becalming after the foregoing trepidation)."[24] This is because conscience can reach one of only two verdicts: guilty or innocent. If the agent is guilty and s/he is not depraved, this will cause him/her pain. But if the agent is innocent, that is no reward; there is no joy that is attendant upon this verdict, at least according to Kant's moral psychology. Thus, this asymmetry in the feelings caused by conscience is related to the asymmetry in the kinds of judgment attributed to conscience (seen earlier): conscience does not judge whether an agent's actions are meritorious.[25]

Although Kant draws a parallel between conscience and a court of law, there is no "statute of limitations" on the judgments issued by conscience, nor is there anything to prevent an agent from feeling the bites of conscience for the same misdeed on more than one occasion. Conscience might judge an agent guilty of having infringed on the moral law for as long as the agent retains a memory of the action. Evidence for this can be found throughout Kant's corpus. For example, in the only mention of conscience in the *Critique of Practical Reason*, Kant suggests that conscientious repentance for a misdeed might

---

[23] To be fair, there are a number of handwritten notes that suggest otherwise. For example, in a note assigned to the period 1764–1768 Kant defines conscience as "the moral feeling applied to one's own actions" (HN, AA 20: 168.10–11), and in a note assigned to the period 1776–1778 Kant writes that the satisfaction or regret one feels regarding the morality of one's action, if felt "before the action," may be called "feeling," but "after the action [it may be called] conscience" (Refl, AA 19: 266.02).

[24] MS, AA 06: 440.30–32.

[25] Despite Kant's claims in his published works that conscience only punishes or reproaches agents for wrongful action, there are a number of notes in which Kant suggests that conscience might have a more positive role to play. For example, in a note from 1776–8 Kant writes that "it appears that rewards everything good and punishes everything evil, but in different degrees" (Refl, AA 19: 266.20–21). Similarly, in a note from 1775–8 Kant writes that "there are two kinds of happy states of mind: 1. Peace of mind or satisfaction (good conscience); 2. The perennially joyous heart" (Refl, AA 15: 260.22–24). He then goes on to say that the first consists in the consciousness that one has behaved in a morally upright fashion, whereas the second is a gift of nature. This has implications for Kant's account of happiness, a topic I discuss in part 3 of Kahn (2019b).

extend long past its occurrence.[26] In retelling the biblical story of Job in the "Miscarriage," Kant has Job declare that "his conscience does not scold him at all for the sake of his entire life."[27] In the *Religion*, Kant repeatedly discusses agents on their deathbeds who engage the faculty of conscience to reflect on misdeeds that might have occurred at any point in their lives.[28] And in the first half of the *Metaphysics of Morals*, Kant asserts that requiring officials to swear an oath at the end of every year (saying that they have fulfilled their official duties faithfully) "would bring conscience more into motion" than requiring them to swear an oath at the beginning of every year (saying that they will do so), reasoning that in the former there will be a cumulative effect associated with failures that will be lacking in the latter.[29]

Kant also thinks that the judgment of conscience might come before an agent's decision to engage in wrongdoing. In the *Metaphysics of Morals*, Kant calls this a "*warning* conscience."[30] This preventive role of conscience is not exactly in keeping with Kant's court metaphor if one thinks that courts require an actual criminal offense (the *actus reus* in the common law tradition). However, that is not an objection to Kant. It merely indicates one of the limits of the court metaphor. Further evidence for ascribing these ideas about the timing of the judgment of conscience to Kant may be found in the students' notes from Kant's lectures, where one finds frequent references to conscience as judging before, during, and after an action, often conjoined with claims about the intensity of this judgment. For example, in one set of notes it is asserted that conscience is most powerful after an action and least powerful during an action.[31]

Thus far I have focused on conscience insofar as it judges whether an agent has infringed on the moral law. However, that is not the only judgment assigned to conscience on Kant's account. Conscience also judges whether an agent has undertaken to determine what his/her duty is with all due diligence. This comes out most clearly in the *Religion*. In the *Religion*, Kant gives two definitions of

---

[26] KpV, AA 05: 098.14–32.   [27] MpVT, AA 08: 265.21–22.

[28] RGV, AA 06: 070.08–14 and 078.27–34.

[29] MS, AA 06: 305.08–09. Kant also thinks that if an agent makes a promise at the beginning of the year, s/he is likely to excuse him/herself later on account of unforeseen difficulties, an excuse that will not be available in retrospect. All of this, of course, rests on generalizations from empirical psychology.

[30] MS, AA 06: 440.11.

[31] V-PP/Herder, AA 27: 043.14–16. However, sometimes it is asserted that conscience is least powerful before an action, of middle power during an action, and most powerful after an action (V-Mo/Collins, AA 27: 356.11–18). And occasionally it is asserted that conscience really only judges at one or another of these times (V-MS/Vigil, AA 27: 617.29–31 seems to suggest that conscience does not judge during an action). So the lecture notes should be handled carefully here.

conscience.[32] According to the first definition, *"conscience is a consciousness which is for itself a duty."*[33] According to the second definition, conscience is *"the moral power of judgment directed toward itself."*[34] To explain his first definition, Kant then argues that (1) "it is a moral principle which requires no proof [that] one should *risk nothing on the danger that it is wrongful*"; thus (2) "of an action that I will to undertake I must not alone judge and opine but rather be certain that it is not wrongful," something Kant calls a "postulate of conscience."[35] To explain his second definition, Kant argues that in conscience, "reason is directed toward itself"; in conscience, reason judges whether it "actually has undertaken the former evaluation of actions with all diligence (whether they [the actions] are right or wrong)."[36] The idea is that it is morally obligatory that an agent be certain that his/her action, in any given case, is permissible, and the faculty of conscience judges whether an agent has fulfilled this obligation with due diligence. Kant calls this moral obligation for certainty the duty of conscience. To put this another way, conscience judges not only whether an agent has fulfilled his/her duties (the first judgment discussed earlier) but also whether an agent has been negligent in determining what his/her duties are (the due diligence judgment).

Kant illustrates all of this with an example. He imagines an inquisitor who is faced with the task of passing judgment on a heretic. Kant then poses the following question:

> now I ask: whether, if he [the inquisitor] sentences him [the heretic] to death, one could say he [the inquisitor] has judged according to his (although erring) conscience, or whether one could give him conscienceless guilt par excellence, whether he might have erred or have done wrong with consciousness.[37]

The issue, according to Kant, is that it is morally certain that taking a life is wrongful, whereas any exemption to this to allow for heretics to be put to death could be based only on revelation and testimony and, as such, "is never apodictically certain."[38] Kant concludes that such an inquisitor cannot merely have erred; his action must have been conscienceless, performed with consciousness of its wrongfulness, for "he would venture to do something in the danger that it is in the highest degree wrong."[39] According to Kant, the

---

[32] However, it should be noted that Kant does not introduce the first as a definition. Rather, much as in section I of the *Groundwork*, when he introduces a second and third proposition in his derivation of the Formula of Universal Law and neglects to say what the first is, Kant introduces his second definition of conscience one paragraph after the first with the remark that "[o]ne could *also* define conscience thusly" (RGV, AA 06: 186.09–10; emphasis mine).

[33] RGV, AA 06: 185.18–19.   [34] RGV, AA 06: 186.10–11.   [35] RGV, AA 06: 185.23–186.07.

[36] RGV, AA 06: 186.16–18.   [37] RGV, AA 06: 186.24–28.   [38] RGV, AA 06: 187.04.

[39] RGV, AA 06: 187.09–10.

inquisitor cannot have carried out the duty of conscience (the duty for moral certitude), for had he done so, he would have realized the error of his ways.

The *Religion* is not the only text where Kant ascribes this due diligence function to conscience. There are various handwritten notes in which Kant says that an agent ought not to perform any action if s/he is uncertain about its deontic status. Probably the most explicit is from 1783–4:

> The supreme principle of conscience is: that nothing is permitted to be done of which the actor is not entirely certain that it (in general) is permitted to be done. We can undertake nothing in the danger of acting wrongfully.[40]

The due diligence function also comes into play in Kant's discussions of the ethics of belief and freedom of conscience.[41] For example, in a draft of the text Kant published in 1798 as *The Conflict of the Faculties*, he says that "what should be counted as religion must be entirely certain . . . for I must answer for it before my conscience."[42] Similarly, in the "Miscarriage" Kant asserts that one commits a wrongful lie if one is negligent in professing to believe something without ascertaining, with all due diligence, that one does:

> Someone thus who says to himself (and, what is the same in matters of religion, before God): he believes, without having cast perhaps even only a glance into himself . . . commits not merely the most incongruous . . . but also the most wrongful lie.[43]

From this it may be seen that, on Kant's account, telling an untruth is not necessary for telling a (wrongful) lie.[44] If one claims to believe something without having engaged in the relevant introspection to determine whether this is so, then one has committed a wrongful lie even if one really does believe it.[45] For example, suppose that someone tracks me down at a conference and asks me, politely if incredulously, whether I really believe the thesis of a paper I published a year before. Pressed for time, I hurriedly but unreflectively reply

---

[40] Refl, AA 18: 579.08–11.

[41] Indeed, the two definitions from the RGV are taken from a section titled "Of the Guiding Thread of Conscience in Matters of Belief" (RGV, AA 06: 185.13).

[42] VASF, AA 23: 436.29–31. Kant's 1783 letter to Moses Mendelssohn is also instructive (Br, AA 10: 347.21–23). In the passage to which this footnote is appended, Kant assumes that religious truths cannot be known with apodictic certainty. This will become important in subsection 2.4.

[43] MpVT, AA 08: 268.22–269.01.

[44] This is borne out in Kant's (in)famous murderer at the door case. In that case, Kant says that telling the murderer that the victim is not at home is wrongful if one does not hold this to be true even if, as a matter of fact, the victim has slipped out of the house (VRML, AA 08: 427.11–20). A similar case can be found in the *Metaphysics of Morals* (MS, AA 06: 431.27–34).

[45] Conversely, Kant thinks that an agent who says something that is literally false has not told a lie if what s/he says is in accordance with his/her best judgment. For a helpful exposition of Kant on lying, see chapter 14 of Wood (2008).

that I do. Finally, suppose that what I said is true and that, if I had reflected sufficiently, I would have realized as much. This, according to Kant, could be an instance of a wrongful lie on account of my lack of introspection. I am going to revisit these ideas about due diligence, introspection, and certainty in subsections 2.3 and 2.4.

Kant's connection between certainty and conscience might be motivated by the fact that the words in German (*gewiss* for certainty, *Gewissen* for conscience) are related.[46] This could help to explain why Kant makes the due diligence function analytic to the concept of conscience (with his *Religion* definitions). The connection also might be motivated by Kant's opposition to probabilism, a doctrine that says that an action is permitted if there is a preponderance of evidence for its permissibility, an evidentiary bar that, on Kant's account, is too low.[47]

However, modern readers might balk at the claim that there is a duty to be certain that one's actions are permissible. Indeed, some might think that such certainty is more frequently conjoined with the most heinous abuses of morality than the alternative. In light of this, it is perhaps worth pointing out that this aspect of Kant's thought is not obviously central to his ethics. For one thing, due diligence need not result in certainty. For another, there are many alternatives between certainty and probabilism: rejection of the latter does not necessitate adoption of the former. I shall return to this in subsection 2.5.

Kant makes different claims about conscience and duty. In some places, Kant claims that there is a duty of conscience. For example, as seen above, Kant's first *Religion* definition of conscience makes the fact that conscience is a duty analytic to the concept of conscience, and he entitles a section of the *Metaphysics of Morals* devoted to a discussion of conscience, "Of the Duty of the Human Being to Himself as the Inborn Judge over Himself."[48] In other places, Kant claims that a duty of conscience is an absurdity. This can be

---

[46] Paton (1979, 248).

[47] Kant's own definition of probabilism is different from the one to which this note is appended. Kant defines probabilism as asserting that "the mere opinion that an action could well be right is already sufficient to undertake it" (RGV, AA 06: 186.08–09). A slightly different definition may be found in the editorial notes to the *Religion* in the Cambridge Edition of the Works of Immanuel Kant. The editors quote the Salamancan Dominican Bartolomeo de Medina, quoted also in the editorial apparatus to the Academy Edition of the *Religion* (RGV, AA 06: 506n186), who defines probabilism as saying that "it is legitimate to follow a *probable* opinion even if there is an opposite and more probable one" (emphasis mine). Hegel, who also rejects probabilism, defines it differently again: "an action is permissible, and may be done with an easy conscience, if the agent can come up with *any* good reason for it, be it only the authority of one theologian, and even if other theologians are known by the agent to dissent ever so widely from that authority" (Hegel, 2008, 140).

[48] MS, AA 06: 437.29–30. Confusingly, this chapter and its immediate predecessor are both labeled as chapter 2.

confusing. But I want to suggest that there is no deep inconsistency or change of position here on Kant's part. Rather, Kant is using similar language to talk about different things. As noted earlier, according to Kant there is a duty of conscience (the duty of conscience) to be certain about the permissibility of one's actions. As will become important in Section 3 of this Element, Kant also thinks that there are conditions in which conscience can and should be "*excited* and *sharpened*."[49]

What Kant thinks is absurd is a duty to create a faculty of conscience from nothing. Kant's argument for this is based on the idea that conscience is the capacity "to recognize duties."[50] As the capacity to recognize duties, conscience is a precondition for having any duties in the first place and, *a fortiori*, of having a duty to create a faculty of conscience.[51] So such a duty would be absurd. I believe this is similar to what Kant has in mind when he writes that if there were a duty to act in accordance with conscience, "there would have to be a second conscience in order to become conscious itself of the act of the first."[52] I believe Kant also has something like this in mind in a note from 1776–8 in which he asserts that conscience "must be an instinct" on the grounds that acts of conscience must not be subordinated to freedom of choice, "for it [conscience] otherwise could exercise no constraint over us."[53] Kant's line of reasoning seems to be that if there were a duty to follow one's conscience, then conscience would have to be entirely under voluntary control, and if conscience were entirely under voluntary control, then an agent simply could switch it off entirely and thereby void the duty to follow his/her conscience to begin with.[54]

From the foregoing, it may be seen that conscience has two main roles in Kant's moral psychology: it judges whether an agent has fulfilled his/her duties, and it judges whether an agent has undertaken to determine his/her duties with due diligence. These judgments can be issued before an action, as a warning: conscience is the faculty whereby an agent recognizes his/her duties. The judgments also can be issued during or after an action. In so doing, conscience can cause an agent to feel pain. But it does not cause an agent to feel positive joy. Kant countenances some kinds of duties of conscience, like cultivating conscience and engaging in due diligence. But other kinds of duties of conscience, like a duty to acquire a conscience or a duty to follow conscience, are absurd. In Section 3 of this Element, I am going to focus on a function of conscience that I have not emphasized here: imputation. I shall argue that, because of the role

---

[49] RGV, AA 07: 078.27–28.   [50] MS, AA 06: 400.26.   [51] MS, AA 06: 399.13–14.
[52] MS, AA 06: 401.16–18.   [53] Refl, AA 19: 266.04–06.
[54] Along the same lines, in the *Metaphysics of Morals* Kant claims that conscience is "an inevitable fact, not obligation and duty" (MS, AA 06: 400.30–31).

conscience plays in judgments about guilt and innocence, conscience is responsible for imputation of both actions and consequences in Kant's ethics, and I shall argue that what Kant says in this context overturns the standard dialectic of the modern moral luck debate.

2.2 Errors

Kant's claims about an erring conscience have attracted a lot of attention in the secondary literature on Kant's theory of conscience.[55] One reason for this might be that it is difficult to figure out what his position is.

In the "Miscarriage," Kant declares that "an erring conscience is a nothing."[56] He repeats this claim verbatim in the *Metaphysics of Morals*.[57] And in the frequent discussions of conscience in the lecture notes, it is claimed that "conscience can never be an error."[58] Kant gives several arguments for this claim. His first argument in the "Miscarriage" is that "if there were such a thing, then one could never be sure of having acted rightly, for even the judge in the last instance could yet err."[59] This argument can be reconstructed as follows: an agent's conscience is the last judge of whether s/he has acted rightly; if the last judge of whether an agent has acted rightly can err, then agents cannot be certain whether they have acted rightly; agents can be certain whether they have acted rightly; therefore an agent's conscience cannot err. From this it may be seen that, according to Kant, the faculty of conscience is infallible in some respect. The question is: in what way is conscience infallible?

As noted in subsection 2.1, on Kant's account, one of the key functions of conscience is to tell an agent whether s/he is guilty of infringing on the moral law. On the basis of this, one might think that the kind of infallibility Kant has in mind has to do with our knowledge of the moral law and the way it applies to a specific situation. The idea would be that an agent's conscience tells an agent what the deontic status of his/her actions are, and such pronouncements cannot be in error. On this interpretation of Kant's claim, an agent's conscientious judgments about the im/permissibility of his/her actions are infallible, for otherwise the agent could not be certain whether s/he has acted rightly. For example, suppose an agent is trying to decide whether it would be permissible to tell a lying promise in order to get some ready money. The agent's conscience warns him/her that this would be impermissible. On the present interpretation of the infallibility of conscience, this warning cannot be mistaken: if an agent's conscience says that action A is im/permissible, then it is so.

---

[55] For a helpful overview, see Kazim (2017, chapter 3).   [56] MpVT, AA 08: 268.10–11.
[57] MS, AA 06: 401.05.   [58] V-MS/Vigil, AA 27: 615.32–36.   [59] MpVT, AA 08: 268.07–13.

If this interpretation is correct, then Kant's "Miscarriage" argument is similar to the extraction argument from the beginning of Meditation III of Descartes' *Meditations on First Philosophy*. In the extraction argument, Descartes maintains that clear and distinct perception is infallible on the grounds that if it were fallible, then the *cogito*, which is known solely through this faculty, would be uncertain. On the present interpretation of Kant, clear and distinct perception is replaced with conscience, and the *cogito* is replaced with judgments about the im/permissibility of a proposed course of action. This kind of infallibility is sometimes attributed to conscience by those who view this faculty as the manifestation or voice of an omniscient deity (in the same way that Descartes views clear and distinct perception as God given).[60] However, this interpretation of Kant's argument is almost certainly mistaken. The best evidence against this interpretation is that Kant asserts explicitly that agents' judgments about the deontic status of their actions can be in error and, more, he does so in close proximity to his claim that conscience cannot err. In the "Miscarriage," Kant says that "I can indeed err in the judgment that I believe to be right."[61] Similarly, in the *Metaphysics of Morals* Kant remarks that "in the objective judgment whether something might be a duty or not one can well sometimes err."[62] And in the student notes there is a helpful discussion that distinguishes between different kinds of error regarding such judgments. The texts distinguish between natural laws and positive laws, and it is claimed that, because natural laws lie in everyone's reason, error regarding the corresponding obligations is always culpable: "only in relation to positive law are there *errores inculpabiles*."[63] So an alternative interpretation of Kant's claim about an erring conscience is called for.

Given that Kant also associates conscience with ideas about due diligence and certainty in ascertaining the deontic status of an action, one might think that this is what he has in mind when talking about the infallibility of an erring conscience. Kant evidently thinks that an agent can err when judging whether an action is im/permissible. But perhaps his denial of an erring conscience has to do with the kinds of second-order judgments agents make about their own

---

[60] I shall return to this kind of infallibility and the idea of conscience as the voice of an omniscient deity in subsection 2.5.

[61] MpVT, AA 08: 268.13–14.   [62] MS, AA 06: 401.05–06.

[63] V-Mo/Collins, AA 27: 355.05–11. Confusion might arise because in some of the student notes, the texts say that an erring conscience is possible. However, it is notable that when they do so, an erring conscience is generally defined as an error in the judgment whether something is a duty. Indeed, in the Collins notes (from which the quotation to which this note is appended is excerpted) it is claimed that "the error of conscience must be 2fold, error *facti et legis*" (V-Mo/Collins, AA 27: 355.01–02). Similarly, in another set of notes it is claimed that "an erring conscience is not a failure of conscience but rather of the understanding" (V-PP/Powalski, AA 27: 198.02–03). Thus, the inconsistency is merely on the surface.

beliefs and internal states (like certainty). On this interpretation, an agent might make a mistake in trying to determine whether it is im/permissible to tell a lying promise to get some ready money (this kind of error is possible). But when this same agent then judges whether s/he actually has employed conscience in order to determine whether this action is im/permissible, this judgment is infallible. The infallibility on this interpretation is in regard to a second-order judgment, like "I believe that S is P" rather than simply "S is P."

This has an air of paradox to it. One might think that there is no difference, for the speaker, between the following three assertions: "I believe that S is P"; "it is true that S is P"; and "S is P." If that is so, then this second interpretation might be thought to collapse back into the first. That is, infallibility about "I believe that S is P" would translate into infallibility about "S is P." To see that these two interpretations are not equivalent, suppose that the speaker is being asked about whether s/he believes in God and recall the excerpt reproduced from the "Miscarriage" in subsection 2.1:

> Someone thus who says to himself (and, what is the same in matters of religion, before God): he believes, without having cast perhaps even only a glance into himself ... commits not merely the most incongruous ... but also the most wrongful lie.[64]

The infallibility that is currently under consideration (with the second interpretation, unlike the first) requires casting a glance into oneself. This means that the judgment that is immune to error takes a different subject (viz., oneself). An agent who conscientiously asserts, "God exists," will be mistaken if there is no God. But that same agent will not be mistaken in asserting, "I believe that God exists," and on this second interpretation of Kant, Kant is saying that conscientious judgments of this latter kind are infallible.

Unlike the first interpretation, this second interpretation is supported by Kant's texts. For example, shortly after his assertion that conscience cannot err in the "Miscarriage," Kant claims that "in the consciousness: *whether I in fact believe* something to be right (or merely profess it), I can absolutely not err, for this judgment, or much more this sentence, merely says: that I judge the object thusly."[65] Similarly, in the *Metaphysics of Morals* Kant clarifies his claim about conscience and error by saying that "in the subjective [judgment] whether I have compared something with my practical (here judging) reason for the purpose of the former judgment [viz., the objective judgment regarding its deontic status] I cannot err."[66]

---

[64] MpVT, AA 08: 268.22–269.01.   [65] MpVT, AA 08: 268.15–18.
[66] MS, AA 06: 401.06–08.

Kant does not intend his assertion of the infallibility of these second-order judgments to rest on a brute appeal to intuition. In the "Miscarriage," he asserts that one can and must stand by such judgments because one is "immediately conscious" of them.[67] Kant's idea seems to be that in judging something about an object ("S is P"), I do so mediately (by means of representations of that object) and, thus, fallibly. By way of contrast, when I judge that I believe something ("I believe that S is P"), I am judging something about my own mental states, so this judgment is not mediated by representations and, therefore, is infallible. In the *Metaphysics of Morals*, Kant asserts that if error about the second-order judgment were possible, "then I would not have judged practically at all; in which case there would be neither error nor truth."[68] In this passage, unlike the "Miscarriage" passage, Kant seems to take for granted that the second-order judgment can fail to be true. Kant's point seems to be that when that occurs (when the second-order judgment is not true), the second-order judgment is not in error, perhaps because error is apt only when a judgment is false, whereas in this case there is something akin to Strawsonian presupposition failure.[69]

On the basis of this, I think it must be admitted that Kant subscribed to infallibility in regard to conscientious judgments of the form "I believe that S is P." However, I also think that Kant's defense of infallibility regarding this kind of second-order judgment is quite weak. The *Metaphysics of Morals* argument, even if successful (and I do not think it is), is at best a verbal quibble. Moreover, Kantian doctrine requires that when I make judgments about my own mental states, I take myself to be not only judging subject but also object judged. So such judgments are not immediate (contra the "Miscarriage"). And even if they were, it is not obvious, at least to me, why such immediacy would preclude error. It is also notable that this kind of infallibility is difficult to sustain in the wake of Freudian ideas about unconscious beliefs. Perhaps there is room for infallibility about conscious-belief-in-the-moment rather than belief-as-dispositional-state. But it is unclear whether this more fleeting notion of a belief would be able to do the work Kant needs it to do in discussing freedom of conscience (the focus of subsection 2.4).

However, the fact that Kant subscribed to this kind of infallibility does not entail that this kind of infallibility is what he is talking about with his claim

---

[67] MpVT, AA 08: 267.30.   [68] MS, AA 06: 401.08–10.

[69] The idea behind Strawsonian presupposition failure can be illustrated by example. Consider the following proposition: "the king of France is bald." If there is no king of France, then a presupposition of this proposition is false. On Russell's analysis, the proposition as a whole is then false, whereas on Strawson's, it is neither true nor false (Beaver and Geurts, 2014, section 5.2).

about the possibility of an erring conscience, and there is another interpretation available. In the first two interpretations advanced here, I have taken "error" to be a theoretical notion about truth and falsity. But one might interpret it as a practical notion instead. On this third interpretation, Kant is saying that an agent's conscience tells an agent whether s/he is guilty of infringing on the moral law, and such pronouncements are determinative in the sense that they are final. That is, on this interpretation, the court of conscience is, like the Supreme Court of the United States, a court of last resort. At a later time, an agent might reject the rule in accordance with which the judgment was made (in the same way that the Supreme Court might reverse an earlier precedent). But whether the agent was guilty in the eyes of the law, the final judgment reached by conscience in that particular case remains unchanged, and there is no further appeal or decision to be made about that instance.

For example, suppose that R is trying to decide whether to kill an old pawnbroker in order to get some ready money. On the one hand, R is in dire straits; the pawnbroker is a louse, sucking the life out of poor people; and R would use the money to do many good deeds. On the other hand, R could earn money in other ways, perhaps by working as a tutor; the pawnbroker is a human being; it is not up to R to mete out punishment for immoral but legal actions; and violence is hateful. Now suppose that R comes to the conscientious judgment that it is permissible to kill the pawnbroker in this case. Finally, suppose that, having reached this conclusion, R takes an axe and does the deed. On the interpretation of Kant's claim about an erring conscience currently under consideration, there is no inconsistency lurking in the fact that R's conclusion about the deontic status of the killing is mistaken.[70] But what is not mistaken or subject to revision is whether, having reached this decision sincerely and conscientiously, R is guilty in the eyes of the (moral) law. Upon seeing the blood and the dead body lying on the ground, R might deeply regret the decision. R might come to the conclusion that killing, especially killing in order to steal, is never permissible and that the earlier judgment was wrong. Others might accuse R of self-deception, duplicity, or worse. But on the current interpretation of Kant's theory of conscience, if R believed, in good conscience, that they were acting permissibly, then that judgment stands as determinative with regard to whether R is innocent or guilty.

---

[70] However, it bears noting that, given Kant's claims about the inquisitor in the *Religion* (discussed earlier), it is doubtful whether he would accept that R's judgment could be conscientious, and Dostoyevsky might side with Kant on this. As I read *Crime and Punishment*, Raskolnikov, on whom this thought experiment is based, wants to reach this judgment conscientiously, to be able to murder for himself and without casuistry. But wanting to do so and actually doing so are two very different things in this context. I would like to thank an anonymous referee for pressing me on this point.

In the next subsection of this Element, I am going to give both direct textual and indirect doctrinal evidence in favor of ascribing this third kind of infallibility to Kant. I also happen to think that this third kind of infallibility, unlike infallibility in regard to second-order judgments about beliefs, is defensible. But is this third kind of infallibility the kind of infallibility Kant has in mind when he talks about the impossibility of an erring conscience? As noted earlier, the first kind of infallibility (infallibility in regard to first-order judgments about the deontic status of actions) is almost certainly not what Kant had in mind. But that leaves open both the second kind of infallibility (infallibility in regard to second-order judgments about one's own beliefs) and the third (infallibility as a practical notion, taking conscience as a court of last resort). At one time, I thought the third interpretation was the correct one.[71] I am no longer sure. However, I see no reason to decide this question here given that there seems to be good evidence for ascribing both kinds of infallibility to Kant independently of his claims about an erring conscience. So rather than try to do so, I turn now to a discussion of Kant on conscientiousness.

2.3 Conscientiousness

Claims that are relevant to Kant's position regarding conscientiousness may be found in all of his major discussions of conscience. Moreover, these claims indicate that Kant's position on this was stable: according to Kant, if an agent has a healthy conscience, then an agent has done all that can be demanded of him/her by the moral law if but only if s/he acts according to conscience. For ease of exposition, I am going to separate this biconditional into two conditionals:

(1) If an agent has acted according to his/her conscience, s/he has done all that the moral law can demand of him/her.

(2) If an agent has done all that the moral law can demand of him/her, then s/he will have acted according to his/her conscience.

In the "Miscarriage," Kant's commitment to (1) is suggested by the way he tells the story of Job. As Kant tells the story, Job has a very good life: he is healthy and wealthy, he has a happy family and good friends, and, more, he is "satisfied with himself in a good conscience."[72] God then takes all of these goods from Job "except for the last [i.e., Job's good conscience]."[73] Job's friends conclude that Job must have sinned against God in some way, otherwise his punishment would be inconsistent with divine justice. Job, however, protests that "his conscience does not scold him at all for the sake of his entire life," and

---

[71] Kahn (2015). [72] MpVT, AA 08: 265.06. [73] MpVT, AA 08: 265.06–07.

so Job instead declares himself "for the system of unconditioned divine decrees."[74] Thus, as Kant tells the story, Job's moral guiltlessness is grounded on the fact that he has a clear conscience.

In the *Religion*, Kant's commitment to (1) is explicit. Kant declares that it is a violation of conscience to profess belief in some religious article of faith despite being conscious that one does not have sufficient evidence for it and only because doing so might enable one to get some reward (or at least to avoid some punishment) in the afterlife. According to Kant, sincerity is the "foundation of conscience," and he thus recommends what he calls a "security maxim" in matters of religious belief: to remain agnostic with regard to anything that can be proven only on the basis of revelation and testimony, even if it is asserted that belief in the thing is a condition of divine grace. Kant thinks that, instead of professing belief in something for which one does not have sufficient evidence, one should try simply not to render oneself unworthy of divine grace through bad conduct or an immoral disposition.[75] Kant avers that in this maxim lies "true moral security, namely before conscience (and more cannot be claimed from a person)."[76] Kant's thoughts about the ethics of belief, as manifested in the security maxim he recommends, will be important in the next subsection of this Element. What is important here is the parenthetical remark stating that not to violate conscience is the most that can be demanded of a person. This demonstrates Kant's commitment to (1) in the *Religion*.

Kant's commitment to (1) is arguably most explicit in the *Metaphysics of Morals*. In the *Metaphysics of Morals*, Kant says that "if however someone is conscious of having acted according to conscience, then nothing more can be demanded from him that concerns guilt or innocence."[77] This claim occurs in such close proximity to Kant's claim that agents can be mistaken in their first-order judgments about the deontic status of an action as to make it unthinkable that he did not realize the implications of the conjunction of these two ideas. Kant is saying, in effect, that such mistakes are irrelevant, at least as far as moral guilt or innocence is concerned. Kant thinks that an agent who makes such an error ought to avail him/herself of the truth insofar as that is possible. But if s/he acted according to conscience (and if his/her first-order judgment is not based on self-serving ratiocination or negligence), then nothing more can be demanded of him/her.

One piece of evidence for ascribing (2) (the converse of (1)) to Kant comes from his claim that an agent must be certain that his/her actions are permissible. As noted in subsection 2.1, in the *Religion* Kant calls this a "postulate of

---

[74] MpVT, AA 08: 265.21–22 and 24.   [75] RGV, AA 06: 190.18–19 and then 189.03–13.
[76] RGV, AA 06: 189.14–15.   [77] MS, AA 06: 401.11–13.

conscience" and "a moral principle that requires no proof."[78] But it follows from this moral principle that if an agent has done all that the moral law can demand of him/her, then s/he will be certain that his/her actions were permissible. And from this and from Kant's account of conscience it follows that if an agent has done all that the moral law can demand of him/her, s/he will have acted in accordance with his/her conscience.

Perhaps an easier way to see this is by contraposition: on Kant's account of conscience, if an agent has not acted in accordance with his/her conscience, s/he cannot be certain that his/her actions were permissible, whence it follows from the postulate of conscience that s/he has not done all that the moral law can demand of him/her. By telescoping these conditionals, we get the contrapositive of (2).

A similar lesson may be drawn from Kant's discussion of false professions in the "Miscarriage." This discussion was used briefly in subsection 2.1 and will become a focal point of the next subsection. The basic message for current purposes is that in his discussion of false professions in the "Miscarriage," Kant seems to suggest that if an agent does not act in accordance with conscience, then s/he has not done all that the moral law can demand of him/her. This, again, is the contrapositive of (2).

Another piece of evidence for ascribing (2) to Kant comes from the way that he defines the term "conscienceless" (*gewissenslos*). In the *Religion* discussion of the inquisitor (reproduced in subsection 2.1), Kant glosses conscienceless-ness as having "done wrong with consciousness."[79] Similarly, in the *Metaphysics of Morals* Kant says that "*consciencelessness* is not lack of conscience but rather a propensity not to turn oneself toward its judgment."[80] For Kant, conscienceless action is not action that is done unwittingly, much less action that is objectively wrong but in accordance with conscience. Rather, conscienceless action is action that is performed while paying no heed to the judgment of conscience (which says that the action is wrong).

The most explicit piece of evidence for ascribing (2) to Kant may be found in the student lecture notes. One of the sets of notes contains a case in which the student is to imagine himself in a place of worship for a religion to which he does not subscribe.[81] As the case is portrayed, the student faces a dilemma: either act against his conscience by prostrating himself before idols he does not believe in, or cause offense to others. According to the notes, the lesson that the students are supposed to learn from consideration of this case is that it is always wrong to act against conscience, even if this means causing offense to others, for

---

[78] RGV, AA 06: 185.23, 186.06–07.   [79] RGV, AA 06: 186.27–28.

[80] MS AA 06: 401.10–11.

[81] My use of the masculine pronoun is not accidental or thoughtless: Kant's students were all male.

my conscience "must be holy to me."[82] From this it follows that if an agent does not act according to conscience (if his/her conscience is not holy to him/her), then s/he will have violated the moral law, the contrapositive of (2).

In addition to direct textual evidence for ascribing (1) and (2) to Kant, there is indirect doctrinal evidence for doing so. In the *Groundwork*, Kant defines his ethics in terms of autonomy. For example, two of the final sections of part II of the *Groundwork* are titled, respectively, "**Autonomy of the Will** *as Supreme Principle of Morality*" and "**Heteronomy of the Will** *as the Source of all Disreputable Principles of Morality*."[83] The reason this is relevant for current purposes is that Kant defines autonomy in terms of giving oneself a law: "Autonomy of the will is the property of the will whereby it is of itself . . . a law to itself."[84] Conversely, heteronomy is defined in terms of seeking a law from some source other than one's own reason: "when the will . . . seeks the law in the property of some one of its objects . . . then *heteronomy* always results."[85] Provided that one has a healthy conscience, to follow the faculty of conscience is to follow one's self-given law, one's fallible but nonetheless best judgment about what the moral law dictates in a given instance. Thus, an argument could be made that (i) to follow conscience is to act autonomously, and (ii) not to follow conscience is to act heteronomously.

From this it may be seen that Kant is committed to the idea, discussed in the last subsection, that conscience is a court of last resort. As noted earlier, this might be what Kant is getting at when he says that an erring conscience is an absurdity. But as also noted earlier, Kant's claim that an erring conscience is an absurdity might also be interpreted in terms of the infallibility of second-order judgments of the form, "I believe that the deontic status of action A is X" (rather than first-order judgments of the form, "the deontic status of action A is X"). Insofar as Kant is committed to both kinds of infallibility independently of his claim about an erring conscience, there does not seem to be a need to decide here which kind he has in mind when he writes that "an erring conscience is a nothing."

It is instructive to contrast Kant's position on conscientiousness with the positions of some of his successors, like Fichte, Fries, and Hegel.[86] Fichte evidently thought that conscience is the ultimate standard of moral behavior and, thus, that if an agent has a healthy conscience, then an agent has done all that can be demanded of him/her by the moral law if but only if s/he acts according to conscience. For example, Fichte claims that

---

[82] V-Mo/Collins, AA 27: 335.24.   [83] GMS, AA 04: 440.14–15, 441.01–02.
[84] GMS, AA 04: 440.16–18.   [85] GMS, AA 04: 441.03–07.
[86] I have benefited here from Wood (1990, chapter 10).

the formal condition for the morality of our actions, or of what properly deserves to be called the morality of the same, consists in deciding to do what conscience demands, purely and simply for conscience's sake. Conscience, however, is *the immediate consciousness of our determinate duty.*[87]

Indeed, one of Fichte's versions of what Kant calls the Categorical Imperative is simply, "Act according to your conscience."[88]

With this in mind, it is unsurprising that Fichte, like Kant, makes conscience a court of last appeal: "Conscience is itself the judge of all convictions and acknowledges no higher judge above itself. It has final jurisdiction and is subject to no appeal."[89] However, Fichte also, but unlike Kant, holds that agents have an "absolute criterion for the correctness of our conviction concerning duty." Indeed, Fichte infers this on the basis of exactly the kind of argument that I asserted should not be ascribed to Kant, a Cartesian extraction argument:

> In order for dutiful conduct to be possible at all there must be an absolute criterion for the correctness of our conviction concerning duty. A certain conviction must be absolutely correct, and for duty's sake we have to stick with this conviction …. But according to the moral law, dutiful conduct is purely and simply possible; therefore, there is such a criterion.[90]

This takes some of the bite out of Fichte's claims about conscience as a court of last appeal.

Fries, like Kant and Fichte, thinks that the "requirements of morality … are pronounced through conscience."[91] Thus, Fries, like Kant and Fichte, seems to think that (1) if an agent has acted according to his/her conscience, s/he has done all that the moral law can demand of him/her, and (2) if an agent has done all that the moral law can demand of him/her, then s/he will have acted according to his/her conscience. But Fries does not think that agents have, through conscience, access to an infallible criterion of the requirements of the moral law. Unlike Fichte but like Kant, Fries thinks that conscience is "capable of education."[92] One thus might expect Fries to appeal to the court of last resort argument that we see in both Kant and Fichte or to Kantian ideas about autonomy. But Fries charts entirely new ground here, maintaining instead that (1) is analytic:

---

[87] Fichte (2005, 164). Fichte makes the same claim again a few pages later: "A command is binding only on the condition that it is confirmed by our own conscience and only *because* it has been confirmed in this way" (Fichte, 2005, 168).

[88] Fichte (2005, 148, emphasis omitted).   [89] Fichte (2005, 165).

[90] Fichte (2005, 156). Fichte makes a similar claim about forty pages later: "In every case, whatever is inner feeling is a duty; and this inner feeling never errs so long as we simply pay heed to its voice" (Fichte, 2005, 197–198).

[91] Fries (1818, 73, emphases omitted).   [92] Fries (1818, 4).

> For the person who has attained purity, "conscience is *infallible*" is an identity, since no more is demanded of anyone than that he truly follow his *pure* conviction. For now conscience only pronounces this conviction, [and] so it always is right in the moment for the individual person in his purity.[93]

That is, according to Fries, the infallibility of conscience is analytic for a person with a healthy conscience ("the person who has attained purity"). Fries' argument for this is based on two conditionals: if an agent follows his/her convictions, then s/he has done all that morally can be demanded of him/her; and if an agent has a healthy conscience, then the pronouncements of conscience are his/her convictions. But it is easy to see that what follows from these two conditionals is that if an agent with a healthy conscience follows his/her conscience, then s/he has done all that the moral law can demand of him/her. So that is evidently what Fries means to affirm when asserting the infallibility of conscience and, more, the analyticity of the same.[94]

Hegel, by way of contrast with Kant, Fichte, and Fries, seems to be much more suspicious of conscience. For example, in *The Phenomenology of Spirit* Hegel spurns those who profess to act according to conscience: "Whoever . . . says that he acts with regard to others according to *his own law* and *his own* conscience is saying in fact that he is mistreating them."[95] Now taken by itself, this might not be thought to have much bearing on whether agents ought to act according to conscience. Rather, Hegel's idea might be that people only feel the need to profess that they are acting conscientiously when they are going to mistreat others. As such, this claim actually presupposes that if an agent follows his/her conscience, then s/he has done all that the moral law can demand of him/her; the problem Hegel is pointing to is that, knowing this, people abuse it, perhaps without sufficient inward reflection on whether they really are acting conscientiously. This interpretation is bolstered by what Hegel says in the very next sentence: "However, *actual* conscience is not this insistence on knowing and willing which opposes itself to the universal; rather, the universal is the element of its *existence*, and its language pronounces its doing as a recognized duty."[96]

But as frequently occurs with Hegel, his position is considerably more complex than this interpretation suggests. For example, consider the following excerpt from the *Outlines of the Philosophy of Right*:

---

[93] Fries (1818, 214–215).

[94] An alternate way to get to the analyticity of (1) on Fries' account: assuming that Fries, like Kant, subscribes to the heritability of syntheticity, it follows that there cannot be a synthetic proposition in the derivation of an analytic one, whence it may be inferred that, according to Fries, (1) is analytic. In this alternate line of reasoning I am also of course assuming that Fries would have been cognizant of what the heritability thesis would imply in this case.

[95] Hegel (2018, 383).   [96] Hegel (2018, 383).

> *Conscience* is the expression of the absolute title of subjective self-consciousness to know in itself and from within itself what is right and obligatory, to give recognition only to what it thus knows as good, and at the same time to maintain that whatever in this way it knows and wills is in truth right and obligatory. Conscience as this unity of subjective knowing with what is in and for itself is a sanctuary which it would be sacrilege to violate. But whether the conscience of a specific individual corresponds with this Idea of conscience, whether what it takes or declares to be good is actually so, is ascertainable only from the *content* of the good it seeks to realize . . . . Conscience is therefore subject to the judgement of its *truth* or untruth, and when it appeals only *to itself* for a decision, it is directly at variance with what it wishes to be, namely the rule for a mode of conduct which is rational, valid in and for itself, and universal.[97]

Hegel distinguishes between the idea of conscience and the conscience of a specific individual. It is only if an individual's conscience corresponds with the idea of conscience that it would be a sacrilege to violate it, and the only way to determine whether an individual's conscience corresponds with the idea of conscience is by means of its specific pronouncements, the content of its moral claims. Thus, the privileged position assigned to conscience by Kant, Fichte, and Fries is decisively rejected by Hegel.[98]

2.4 Belief and Testimony

Fully to appreciate the ways Kant brings conscience to bear on issues related to belief and testimony requires some historical background.[99] In 1786, Frederick the Great, who had ruled Prussia since 1740, passed away. He was succeeded by Frederick William II. History texts often portray these two as polar opposites, especially, and importantly for present purposes, with regard to their attitudes toward the enlightenment credo of thinking for oneself. Whereas Frederick the Great had been a patron of the enlightenment, Frederick William II sought to curb its freethinking opposition to authority, in part by censorship and enforced religious conformity.

The shift in power did not initially have much impact on Kant. Indeed, when Frederick William II visited Königsberg shortly after taking office, Kant was singled out, but he was singled out for special favor rather than disfavor, and he was made a corresponding member of the Berlin Royal Academy of Sciences soon thereafter. This is all the more remarkable given that in 1781 Kant had

---

[97] Hegel (2008, 133).

[98] I would like to thank Howard Williams for encouraging me to think this through.

[99] The brief narrative here is based on that found in the general introduction to the volume on *Religion and Rational Theology* in the Cambridge Edition of the Works of Immanuel Kant as well as the translator's introduction to the "Miscarriage" in that volume.

published the first edition of the *Critique of Pure Reason*, a work characterized as "all-destroying" in part because of its assault on traditional proofs of God's existence. But things changed quickly. In 1788, Frederick William II appointed a new Minister of Education and Religious Affairs, a man named J. C. Wöllner. Wöllner thereupon announced, among other things, that any existing clergy who gave grounds for doubting their adherence to religious doctrine would be dismissed, and, in addition, that new appointments would be conditional on the appointee not having given any grounds for questioning the same. Wöllner also established a commission that would report immediately to Frederick William II and that would be responsible for censoring all publications on religion and morality that came out in Berlin. In 1790, that same commission set up a new system for testing theology students. The new system involved both a rigorous examination to ensure knowledge of church doctrine and an oath testifying adherence to and belief in this doctrine.

Kant knew about and was not pleased with these developments, and the reason they are so important for current purposes is that they serve as the backdrop for his first extended remarks on conscience in print: one of the themes of the 1791 "Miscarriage," made explicit in the concluding section but also present in the main text, is the moral vice of insincerity qua violation of conscience, especially in the form of false professions of faith elicited by fear or self-interest. However, the story does not end with the "Miscarriage." In 1791, the same year that the "Miscarriage" was published, the first essay of the four-part *Religion* was submitted to the censors. It was approved on the grounds that, like most of Kant's work, it dealt with philosophical issues and was intended only for the learned. The second essay, submitted later that year, was not so lucky. The censorship commission deemed it theological rather than philosophical and rejected it on the grounds that it was heterodox. Kant's publisher appealed the rejection, but the appeal was also rejected. This serves as the backdrop for Kant's second extended remarks on conscience in print: one of the themes of the fourth essay of the *Religion*, published in 1793, is, again, false professions of faith and, more, forced professions of faith. But how was this fourth essay published when the second one was blocked?

Kant was not content to let his work lie fallow. Instead of publishing the *Religion* in separate installments as he initially had planned, Kant put them together into a book. He then, first, submitted the manuscript to the theological faculty at the University of Königsberg (where he was employed) to get an independent judgment regarding whether the text fell within the ambit of the theological faculty or the philosophical faculty and, second, upon receiving the judgment he wanted (that his work should be judged by philosophers rather than theologians), proceeded to submit the manuscript to the philosophy faculty at the University of Jena for judgment regarding whether it was appropriate for publication. The philosophy faculty deemed the book appropriate, and Kant accordingly took his manuscript, along with its newly acquired imprimatur, to a publisher; it came out as a book in 1793.

In proceeding as he did, Kant's actions were perfectly legal: the law allowed for university work to be judged by university faculty (rather than the official censorship commission), and by putting his four essays together in a book, Kant effectively had made his text into university work. Moreover, Kant had been under no obligation to submit his second essay to the censors in the first place. The periodical to which he had submitted it recently had moved out of Berlin and so was outside the jurisdiction of the censorship commission (indeed, the periodical had relocated for precisely this reason). But given that he already had received a hard "no" from the censors, Kant could not have been surprised when, in 1794 (after publishing yet another essay in which, as in the "Miscarriage," he leveled barbs against these selfsame censors), Kant received a royal edict singling out the *Religion* in particular, asking him to account for his actions, and forbidding him from further publishing on religion. In response, Kant maintained that his work was primarily philosophical rather than theological and, as such, could not do any harm to religion or public order. But he nonetheless promised not to publish on religious topics anymore, a promise he faithfully kept until the death of Frederick William II in 1797.[100]

This historical background adds a layer of depth to Kant's remarks about forced professions of faith, remarks that are relevant to this Element because they are tied directly to the faculty of conscience. For example, in the *Religion* Kant reflects on whether it would be permissible for someone in a position of authority to require people, on pain of "loss of their position," to profess belief in some religious truth.[101] According to Kant, anybody who forces others to make such professions (professions of things that are not known with apodictic certainty) must be acting against his/her conscience:

> His spiritual superior would hereby, contrary especially to conscience, guide others to profess to believe something which he himself never can be fully convinced of.[102]

Similarly, a few pages later in the *Religion* Kant argues that it is a gross violation of conscience "to demand such a declaration of faith, which allows no

---

[100] After Frederick William II died, his censorship rules were rolled back by his successor. Kant thereupon reasoned that his promise had been to the particular individual rather than to the throne as such, and he thus took his promise no longer to be binding. In section 3 of Kahn (2019a) I give grounds for thinking that this reasoning is inconsistent with Kantian ethics.
[101] RGV, AA 06: 187.19.   [102] RGV, AA 06: 187.30–33.

limitation, and to label the temerity of such protestations even itself as a duty and serviceable to God."[103]

These claims are probably partly what got Kant into trouble with the ruling authorities. Given the context just outlined, it is hard not to read this aspect of Kant's theory of conscience as a direct attack on what Kant viewed as the benighted policies that recently had been enacted, an attack Kant repeated even after the policies had been discarded. In the first half of the *Metaphysics of Morals*, Kant says that a judge in a court of law who requires someone to swear that some belief is true "commits a great offense against the conscientiousness of the affiant."[104] Kant's argument in the *Metaphysics of Morals*, like his argument in the *Religion*, hinges on the fact that the forced professions he is talking about (professions of faith in religious doctrines) cannot be known with certainty. In the *Metaphysics of Morals*, Kant's argument against forced professions is that (i) the point of distinguishing belief from knowledge is that the former is not certain and, thus, by definition, not something that one properly can swear to; (ii) the affiant might realize, the next day (when contemplating from a different perspective), that his/her belief is unjustified and thus will feel bites of conscience when reflecting on the fact that s/he swore otherwise; and (iii) the judge's compelling the agent to swear such an oath will cause a state of thoughtlessness that will preclude him/her from realizing any of this at the time.[105]

One might think that, given how I have reconstructed Kant's argument, the violation of conscience is on the side of the affiant rather than on the side of the authority compelling the profession of belief. But that is not so. For Kant, the violation of conscience is on both sides. Or, to be more precise, for Kant, the

---

[103] RGV, AA 06: 190.02–04.   [104] MS, AA 06: 305.21–24.

[105] In an unpublished note from 1785–8 Kant similarly claims that professions of faith are "a burden for conscience" (Refl, AA 18: 602.21). But his argument in the note seems to be built on the transitory nature of belief rather than on the uncertainty associated with belief: in the note Kant says that someone can swear to believe something now, but s/he cannot swear always to believe something. This seems to be in keeping with Kant's "Miscarriage" position (echoed in the *Metaphysics of Morals*) that an agent cannot be in error regarding judgments of the form "I believe that S is P" (perhaps Kant's considered position is that I cannot be in error about such judgments only if they are indexed to the present).

Kant seems to appeal to the transitoriness of belief in the second premise of my reconstruction of the *Metaphysics of Morals* forced professions argument. So it is possible that Kant intended to make two arguments against forced professions in the *Metaphysics of Morals*, one based on the transitoriness of belief and one based on the uncertainty of (mere) belief. It is also possible that Kant would not have viewed these two arguments as independent of one another. For example, if Kant took the certainty of a belief to be at odds with the transitoriness of that belief, that could serve as a bridge principle between the two arguments.

I am not going to attempt to settle these issues. The point for present purposes is that Kant objected to forced professions of faith on the grounds that to elicit such professions is to force someone into a violation of conscience.

judge violates conscience because the judge is compelling the affiant to violate conscience. As Kant explains later in the *Metaphysics of Morals*:

> To ensure that someone not meet this inner reproach [of conscience] deservedly is now indeed even not *my* duty but rather *his* business; however [it *is* my duty] to do indeed nothing which, according to the nature of the person, could be a temptation to that whereby his conscience can afterwards plague him, [to do indeed nothing] which one calls a scandal.[106]

Kant says here that I have no duty to ensure that others do not deservedly reproach themselves via conscience for failing to follow the moral law. But he says that I nonetheless do have a duty not to tempt them to commit actions for which they will reproach themselves later. This is the duty violated by the judge in the *Metaphysics of Morals* and the spiritual authority in the *Religion*: in eliciting forced professions, they are tempting the agent to act in a way that s/he will reproach him/herself for later (because later, when considering things from a different perspective, the agent will realize that his/her belief is quite uncertain). So on Kant's account, forcing someone to make a profession of faith is a violation of conscience, and it is so because it forces the affiant to violate his/her conscience.

One thing that is notable about this is that Kant's position is consistent with forced professions of things that are known with apodictic certainty, like 2+2=4 (and, for Kant, "every event has a cause" and "rational nature exists as an end in itself"). This is notable because it serves to highlight, in a way not frequently remarked upon, the importance for Kant of the fact that the reasons for belief in God are, according to him, sufficient merely for moral purposes and not for apodictic certainty. However, Kant's theism (and how it relates to his theory of conscience) will be the focus of the next subsection of this Element. For now, I turn to the reason why Kant thinks that a forced profession would involve the affiant in a violation of conscience.

In the "Miscarriage," Kant distinguishes two kinds of conscientiousness: material conscientiousness and formal conscientiousness. According to Kant, "material [conscientiousness] consists in the watchfulness of venturing nothing in the danger that it might be wrong: in contrast to this, [formal conscientiousness] consists in the consciousness of having exercised this watchfulness in a given case."[107] He then elaborates on formal conscientiousness, which is said to consist in the care one exercises in becoming conscious of one's belief and "professing no affirmation of something" in the absence of this consciousness.[108] It is on these grounds that Kant asserts (as seen earlier) that a failure to be truthful (rather than

---

[106] MS, AA 06: 394.03–10.   [107] MpVT, AA 08: 268.07–10.
[108] MpVT, AA 08: 268.19–22.

a failure to tell the truth) is the most wrongful lie. It is also on these grounds that, when telling the story of Job, Kant criticizes Job's friends.

According to Kant, Job's friends, in professing the justice of Job's punishment, fail in conscientiousness. Despite having no hard evidence of Job having sinned, Job's friends infer that he must have done so on the basis of a prior commitment to God's omnibenevolence.[109] But Kant thinks that, in the absence of any such hard evidence, Job's friends cannot really believe this inference.[110] And because (as seen earlier) Kant thinks it is possible by means of conscience to determine infallibly what one believes, Kant interprets Job's friends as being insincere: as attempting to curry favor from a watching deity who has the power to reward them for their abject devotion.[111] This was probably intended as a swipe at those who complied with the recent decrees discussed earlier. But it also reveals why Kant thinks that forced religious professions involve the affiant in a violation of conscience. As seen in subsection 2.3, one of the essential marks of conscience, for Kant, is that it can determine infallibly whether one believes something. But Kant thinks that the content of religious professions cannot be apodictically certain. So a forced religious profession requires an affiant to be untruthful, in violation of what s/he can determine infallibly by means of conscience.

Kant makes similar claims in the *Religion*. As noted in subsection 2.3, in the *Religion*, Kant declares that religious professions in the absence of sufficient evidence are a violation of conscience. According to Kant, there cannot be sufficient evidence in such matters, so such professions are bound to be insincere. It is in this context that Kant contrasts two different kinds of "security maxim" in regard to belief. The first such maxim Kant considers is:

> If that which I avow of God is true, then I have hit the mark; if it is not true, [and] anyway also nothing in itself impermissible: then I have believed it merely superfluously, which indeed was not necessary, [and] however only for example a complaint, which nevertheless is no outrage, can be laid upon me.[112]

This line of reasoning resembles Pascal's wager, and Kant probably means to attribute it to those who comply with Wöllner's edicts. Kant thinks that an agent

---

[109] MpVT, AA 08: 265.14–20.

[110] Kant's reasoning here does not sit well with his theory of conscience. Kant remarks approvingly of Job that the latter "did not ground his morality on belief but rather his belief on morality" (MpVT, AA 08: 267.10–11). But if someone were convinced that s/he had good theoretical grounds for belief in God's omnibenevolence, then an inference from divine punishment to moral wrongdoing could be warranted even in the absence of empirical grounds for wrongdoing. And it is manifestly possible, on Kant's theory of conscience, for someone to be convinced of this.

[111] MpVT, AA 08: 265.29–266.02.   [112] RGV, AA 06: 188.14–17.

who acts on this maxim would be "giving out something, even before God, for certain, [something] whereof he himself is nevertheless conscious that, by its nature, it is not [something] to affirm with unconditioned confidence."[113] The reason this is specifically tied to conscience for Kant is, again, that he thinks that an agent's conscience can determine infallibly whether s/he believes something with certainty. Because the subject of these professions cannot ("by its nature") be known with certainty, to profess otherwise is necessarily to violate conscience.[114]

The second security maxim Kant considers is the one discussed in subsection 2.3:

> Whatever, as means or as condition of happiness, can be avowed by me, not through my own reason, but rather only through revelation, and can be taken up in my confession alone by means of a historical belief, but does not anyway contradict the pure principles of morality, I can indeed not believe and attest for certain, but also even so little disavow as certainly false. At the same time, without determining anything about this, I reckon on the fact that whatever salvific may be contained therein will come to good to me insofar as I do not make myself unworthy of it, for example through a paucity of the moral disposition in a good lifestyle.[115]

This maxim, which is the one Kant recommends, is to believe only on the basis of sufficient evidence. Kant thinks that, rather than believe in the face of Pascal's wager, one should act so as to render oneself worthy of whatever goods this belief is supposed to garner. Kant's favored security maxim serves to tie his ideas about the violation of conscience involved in false professions to a more fundamental violation of conscience involved in believing on the basis of insufficient evidence. Kant sometimes talks about this as inner professions before God. So the connection between an affiant's wrongdoing in forced professions and an individual's wrongdoing in believing (professing internally) on insufficient evidence is, for Kant, quite close. In both cases, one is professing contra conscience, professing what is necessarily contra conscience. And that, of course, is wrongful.

One last thing. Before turning to Kant's theism, I want to note that the discussion here should give pause to those who would associate with Kant extreme views on the impermissibility of lying. Given the historical background against which Kant was writing, he was (understandably) very concerned with

---

[113] RGV, AA 06: 188.19–189.02.

[114] As with Kant's claims about Job's friends, Kant's attribution of this maxim to and consequent condemnation of Wöllner's affiants is difficult to reconcile with Kant's own theory of conscience (see note 110).

[115] RGV, AA 06: 189.04–13.

issues related to freedom of conscience. Realizing that this is what he was writing about can help modern-day readers, most of whom do not face anything like the kind of forced religious conformity Kant witnessed, to make better sense of Kant's views. I shall return to this in the next subsection.

2.5 Theism

As noted in subsection 2.1, in a discussion of the trinity in the *Religion*, Kant takes the judgments of conscience to be the judgments of God as the Holy Spirit. In the *Religion*, Kant makes this connection between conscience and God by means of a practical argument for the existence of God. The argument begins with the concept of the highest good (HG), and for that reason I shall call it the HG argument for the existence of God. Kant articulates the HG argument for the existence of God repeatedly throughout his corpus. One of the things that makes the argument challenging and interesting for historians is that there are subtle differences in these different articulations. For the sake of simplicity (and because this is not an exploration of the HG argument but rather of Kant's theory of conscience), I am going to confine myself to the version of the argument found in the *Critique of Practical Reason*.

The HG is a world in which agents are supremely virtuous and in which they enjoy a degree of happiness in proportion to their virtue.[116] According to Kant, we have a duty to promote such a world.[117] However, Kant also thinks that such a world is an objective possibility only if God exists, we have immortal souls, and we are transcendentally free.[118] The idea seems to be that, although the HG is logically possible in itself, it can have a ground in reality (and thus it can be rational to pursue the HG as an end) only if God, immortal souls, and transcendental freedom are real: God is required in order to ensure that the laws of nature promise happiness in proportion to virtue; immortality is required in order to ensure the infinite amount of time needed to attain perfect virtue; and transcendental freedom is required in order to ensure the ability to act morally in the first place.[119]

Because the HG is an objective possibility only if these three conditions (God exists, we have immortal souls, and we are transcendentally free) are satisfied, Kant maintains that the duty to promote the HG generates a warrant or permission to believe in these things.[120] Kant does not want to argue that morality generates truth-conducive evidence for these beliefs.[121] Rather, his argument seems to trade on something like a pragmatic encroachment theory of

---

[116] KpV, AA 05: 110.12–111.05.　　[117] KpV, AA 05: 144.33–34.
[118] KpV, AA 05: 144.34–35.　　[119] KpV, AA 05: 132.19–29.
[120] KpV, AA 05: 134.08–135.13.　　[121] KpV, AA 05: 135.13–27.

justification: instead of providing evidence, the presence of a duty lowers the bar of justification so that less evidence is required to justify belief, at least for the purposes of fulfilling this duty.[122] Thus, on Kant's account, theoretical certainty is not required in order for agents to be justified when it comes to belief in God, immortal souls, and transcendental freedom. In order to mark the fact that the justification for these three beliefs is different in kind from the justification required for beliefs in theoretical philosophy, Kant calls them practical postulates.[123]

I am primarily interested in the HG argument for the existence of God (rather than immortality or transcendental freedom) because this argument has some important points of contact with Kant's theory of conscience. The first point of contact between Kant's HG argument and his theory of conscience has to do with his claims about the certainty required for an action to be permissible (reproduced in subsection 2.1). In an extended discussion in the *Critique of Pure Reason* about the difference between having an opinion, believing, and knowing, Kant argues, on the one hand, that belief in God is warranted in light of the HG argument despite a paucity of truth-conducive evidence, but, on the other hand, that certainty in moral and mathematical judgments is required in light of the fact that these are judgments of pure reason.[124] Two things follow from this: (a) Kant's certainty requirement does not apply to all judgments (e.g., it does not apply to the practical postulates); and (b) Kant's certainty requirement does not apply only to judgments about the deontic status of actions an agent is about to perform (it applies also to mathematical judgments).[125]

---

[122] KpV, AA 05: 142.18.143.04.   [123] KpV, AA 05: 142.04–06.

[124] KrV, A820–A831/B848–B859; AA 03: 531–538. I have simplified Kant's account in the sentence to which this note is appended: in discussing the (subjective) justification for belief in God in this passage, Kant also refers to physicotheology and the utility of belief in a purposive creator in relation to theoretical investigation of the world.

[125] Even though my aim in this section of the Element is primarily exegetical, I want to suggest that Kant's certainty requirement for judgments about the deontic status of an action an agent is going to perform should be discarded. There are at least three reasons for this. First, this certainty requirement does not sit well with Kant's claims about the possibility of error in judgments about the deontic status of an action: one might think that, given the possibility of such error, a possibility that agents surely are capable of being cognizant of, agents never should be absolutely certain about such judgments. Second, Kant's proposal about certainty also does not sit well with the kind of modesty and humility that plausibly would be recommended by his own theory in the face of interpersonal disagreement about moral judgments. Third and finally, Kant's certainty requirement does not sit well with the exigencies of life: agents frequently are placed in situations in which they have no choice but to act in the face of uncertainty – situations in which a certainty requirement would be paralyzing or worse. Rejecting Kant's certainty requirement, however, raises an immediate puzzle: what should be put in its place?

I am not able to solve this puzzle here. But I do want to say a few words about it. As noted in subsection 2.1, I think that Kant's certainty requirement is bound up with his claims about the due diligence function of conscience. But it seems to me that certainty is less important than due diligence; that due diligence need not result in certainty; and that the amount of diligence that is

The second point of contact, noted in the opening paragraph of this subsection, has to do with God as a divine lawgiver and the idea of duties as divine commands: "the moral law leads, through the concept of the highest good . . . to religion, i.e. to the cognition of all duties as divine commands."[126] The structure of Kant's argument here can be reconstructed in two steps: (a) from the duty to promote the highest good, infer the existence of God; and (b) from the existence of God, move to considering duties as divine commands.

However, in the *Metaphysics of Morals*, Kant makes a different argument for belief in God. Kant claims in the *Metaphysics of Morals* that "the conscience of a human, with all duties, will have to think of *another* (than the human as such, that is) than himself to be judge of his actions."[127] Kant then argues that (i) because the court of conscience is internal, this other must know the true moral character of a person; (ii) because conscience is the judge of all free actions, this other must be all-obliging; (iii) because such a moral being must be able to mete out an effect corresponding to these obligations, this other must be omnipotent; (iv) "but such a moral being that also has power over everything is called **God**."[128] On the basis of this, Kant infers that conscience generates

---

due in a given case will depend on (among other things) the kind and severity of the potential duty that an agent takes to be at stake. An analogy might be helpful to illustrate what I have in mind. In trying to determine what course of treatment to prescribe for a patient, a medical doctor should do his/her due diligence, which might include taking a medical history and conducting various tests. The amount of diligence that is due in a given case will be a function of his/her resources (time, equipment, money, etc.), and it also will be a function of the severity of the consequences of a mistake. For example, a patient who presents with a problem that seems relatively innocuous might secure very quickly and with little hassle a prescription for a cheap drug that is known to have little chance of causing harm. The drugs required to commit physician-assisted suicide, by way of contrast, are much more heavily regulated: in many places where physician-assisted suicide is legal, multiple interviews with specialists are required in order to demonstrate soundness of mind, and in some places a patient must demonstrate that s/he has a terminal illness.

The point I am trying to make is that something similar might hold for the diligence required in determining the deontic status of an action: the diligence that is due might be a function of (a) how much time the agent has to think and interrogate him/herself (and others) and (b) the severity, so to speak, of the duty. An example might be drawn from Kant's casuistical questions in the *Metaphysics of Morals*. After discussing the duty not to lie, Kant asks whether "an untruth out of mere politeness . . . can be held for a lie?" He illustrates this with the way that his contemporaries often would end their letters, writing something like "your obedient servant" before signing their names (MS, AA 06: 431.17–18). The way that Kant poses this question (and many others like it in the corresponding sections of casuistical questions following the derivations of other general duties in the *Metaphysics of Morals*) suggests that he takes it to be genuinely open for discussion, not obvious one way or another. And what I have in mind is that the due diligence requirement to determine whether such an untruth is permissible (ending a letter with the expression "your obedient servant," even if not sincerely meant) is not as rigorous as the corresponding requirement that would be associated with determining, for example, whether dropping the first atom bomb in World War II was permissible.

[126] KpV, AA 05: 129.16–19, emphases omitted.   [127] MS, AA 06: 438.33–36.
[128] MS, AA 06: 439.03–13.

a subjective warrant for belief in God insofar as it points agents toward thinking of their duties as divine commands. I am going to call this the conscience argument for the existence of God.

The conscience argument for the existence of God is very different from the HG argument for the existence of God. One difference is that the concept of the HG is absent from the conscience argument. A deeper difference is that the inferential structures of the arguments are reversed.[129] Whereas (as noted earlier) in the HG argument Kant moves from the existence of God to divine command, in the conscience argument Kant moves in the opposite direction, from divine command to the existence of God. Moreover, to judge from the student notes, Kant made frequent use of the conscience argument in his lectures. For instance, in one set of notes it is claimed that conscience "appears to be the cause of why man believes in god";[130] in another, that conscience is "the representative of the divine forum";[131] and in yet another, that the reproaches of conscience would be "without effect if one did not think of it as the representative of God."[132]

On the basis of this, Kant might be thought to have two practical arguments for the existence of God: (i) the HG argument for the existence of God and (ii) the conscience argument for the existence of God. This already upsets the standard picture of Kant, which takes account only of (i).[133] But I want to suggest that Kant's *Metaphysics of Morals* conscience argument marks an important but neglected stepping stone in the evolution of his thought, an evolution that ultimately sees him giving up on the HG argument for the existence of God: after tinkering with it for about twenty years and in multiple publications, unpublished notes, and (to judge from the student lecture notes) lectures, Kant put the HG argument down around 1800 in favor of the conscience argument, and the *Metaphysics of Morals* represents a transition point in that development.

---

[129] This is important because it foils attempts to amalgamate the two arguments.

[130] V-PP/Powalski, AA 27: 197.20–21.   [131] V-Mo/Collins, AA 27: 297.22–23.

[132] Päd, AA 09: 495.05–06. This excerpt is from the *Pedagogy* material found in volume 9 of the Academy Edition. The *Pedagogy* material is different from the other sets of lecture notes. This material was written up by one of Kant's colleagues, Rink, at Kant's behest and on the basis of notes that Kant himself had written for use in giving lectures. The text has been translated in the Cambridge Edition anthology titled *Anthropology, History, and Education*, and this short note is based on the introduction found therein.

[133] A further problem for the standard picture stems from the fact that Kant thinks that there are theoretical grounds for believing in God. For example, in the *Critique of Practical Reason* Kant asserts that consideration of the "order, purposiveness, and magnitude" of the world warrants an inference to the existence of a *"wise, good, powerful, etc."* creator, even if our limited experience does not warrant an inference to the existence of an omniscient, omnibenevolent, omnipotent, etc. creator (KpV, AA 05: 139.20–24).

The primary evidence for Kant's having given up the HG argument for the existence of God comes from the *Opus Postumum*, an unpublished set of handwritten notes from the end of Kant's life. The first and seventh convolutes of the *Opus Postumum* are usually taken to have been written after 1800, and in these convolutes Kant repeatedly makes claims like this one: "God is quite simply: I take it upon my conscience, when I speak untruthfully, to call [myself] a liar."[134] This is a restatement of the conscience argument, not the HG argument. Moreover, in many restatements of this argument, Kant says that it is the only argument for belief in God: "There is only one practical//sufficient argument for belief in a God ... the cognition of all human duties as (*tanquam*) divine commands." This can be read as a disavowal of the HG argument for the existence of God.[135]

Rather than dwell on this point about the historical evolution of Kant's thought, I want to close out this section by gesturing toward a problem for both of Kant's practical arguments for the existence of God that stems from his theory of conscience. Consider the following three claims:

(1) Conscience should be interpreted as the voice of God.
(2) Conscience is infallible.
(3) God is infallible.

Kant is committed to (1) on both practical arguments for the existence of God; the difference between the arguments is in the role (1) plays (whether it is a conclusion of the argument, as in the HG argument, or whether it is a premise of the argument, as in the conscience argument), not in whether Kant is committed to it. As seen in subsections 2.2 and 2.3, Kant also is committed to (2), and he is so in two distinct ways: Kant thinks that conscience judges infallibly whether I believe something, and Kant thinks that conscience is a court of last resort. Finally, Kant is also committed to (3) as a traditional part of the Judeo-Christian-Islamic tradition.

The trouble that arises now is that Kant is not committed to (2) in a way that makes it consistent with (1) and (3). In particular (and as seen in subsection 2.2), Kant thinks that agents can err in judging the objective moral status of an action. Kant also thinks that agents are frequently (perhaps always) unable to determine the maxims underlying their actions. This, conjoined with (1), would entail that God's judgments about the deontic status of actions and about our moral innocence and guilt are fallible, contradicting (3). Further problems arise when one considers that, according to Kant, conscience requires training (and

---

[134] OP, AA 21: 148.23–24.
[135] OP, AA 22: 127.12–14. I discuss this at greater length in Kahn (2018).

that it can be trained poorly). Whether these problems can be solved is not something I can explore here.

3 Kantian Ethics

As noted in Section 1, this section of the Element is philosophical. In parallel with Section 2, I have divided this section of the Element into five subsections. In subsection 3.1, I make some remarks about how Kant's theory of conscience bears on moral training. In subsection 3.2, I take a critical look at the non-accidental rightness condition. In subsection 3.3, I show how Kant's theory of conscience can be brought to bear on moral luck. In subsection 3.4, I examine the guise of the objectively good thesis. In subsection 3.5, I look at some puzzle cases that arise from Kant's theory of conscience.

3.1 Moral Training

Kant's ethics frequently is characterized as concerned exclusively with assessing agents' actions. It is characterized as doing so solely by means of the intentions and principles underlying these actions. One frequent complaint that is then raised against Kant's ethics is that, unlike virtue ethics, Kant's ethics is unable to take into consideration character, training, and moral education.[136] This characterization is perhaps unsurprising when one considers that (1) the goal of the *Groundwork* is to find the Supreme Law of Morality and (2) for many, the *Groundwork* is their only familiarity with Kant. Nonetheless, this characterization is grossly mistaken. There is a growing body of Kant scholars who have engaged to correct this error. But as far as I am aware, none has appealed to Kant's theory of conscience to do so. I aim to begin to correct that lacuna here.

In one of the sets of lecture notes it is claimed that "conscience is natural, but one must cultivate attentiveness to its judgment."[137] This aligns with the interpretation suggested earlier for reconciling Kant's conflicting claims regarding whether there are duties of conscience: some kinds of duties of conscience are incoherent (there can be no duty to acquire a faculty of conscience whole cloth), whereas others make good sense. In this case, there is a duty to cultivate this natural faculty and to become more attentive to its voice. This is affirmed in Kant's published texts. For example, in the *Metaphysics of Morals* Kant claims that every agent has a duty "to cultivate his conscience, to sharpen the

---

[136] A second complaint is then that, unlike consequentialism, Kant's ethics is unable to take into consideration the consequences of agents' actions. This second complaint will become relevant in subsection 3.3.

[137] V-PP/Powalski, AA 27: 198.15–17.

attentiveness to the voice of the inner judge and to use every means (hence only indirect duty) in order to gain a hearing for it."[138]

There are at least two ways in which the training of conscience can go awry. There is something Kant refers to in the *Metaphysics of Morals* as "Micrology" or "fantastic virtue."[139] An agent's conscience is said to be micrological when it treats actions that are morally indifferent as if they were obligatory or forbidden, "when it is exacting in relation to that which is not moral."[140] In the lecture notes there also is discussion of the inverse of this, "Latitudinarius," a condition that "makes the gates to heaven so wide that it also lets through immoral actions."[141]

Kant's remarks in the *Religion* suggest one way in which Latitudinarius might be induced. Kant imagines someone on their deathbed and reflecting on their past actions. Kant argues that summoning a member of the clergy in such a situation in order to provide comfort on account of "the reproaches of conscience" is counterpurposive.[142] At such a time conscience "should rather be *excited* and *sharpened*."[143] Indeed, Kant goes so far as to say that if one instead were "to give opium for conscience" in the form of such comforting, one would be acting "contrary to what is owed to [the person] himself and to others, those who outlive him."[144]

Apparently, the way to administer opium to conscience is to try to convince the agent that his/her past misdeeds were not really so bad, either because there were mitigating conditions present that excuse the agent or because the magnitude of the evil was not so great after all. Implicit in Kant's discussion is that this kind of dulling of conscience can take place at any time in a person's life and that, like the pain-relieving effects of opioids, the pain-relieving effects of this kind of ratiocination might wear off. Obviously, this kind of ratiocination can be entirely first-personal. However, one thing that is notable about the *Religion* discussion is that Kant recognizes that it also can be second-personal. Moreover, Kant declares that there is, as with forced professions of faith, a duty not to elicit this kind of ratiocination in others.

Kant's remarks in the *Religion* also suggest how to avoid Latitudinarius, at least in someone who is on their deathbed:

> If however one is worried that his reason will judge him too mildly through
> conscience, then one errs, I believe, greatly. This is so on precisely these

---

[138] MS, AA 06: 401.19–21.   [139] MS, AA 06: 409.13–19.

[140] V-PP/Powalski, AA 27: 199.34–36.

[141] V-PP/Powalski, AA 27: 200.11–15. A delicate conscience, by way of contrast, is one "which in no way lets through actions which appear to be an overstepping of morality without giving them over to the judge" (V-PP/Powalski, AA 27: 200.15–17).

[142] RGV, AA 06: 078.27.   [143] RGV, AA 06: 078.27–28.   [144] RGV, AA 06: 078.33–34.

grounds: because it [reason] is free and ought itself to speak about him, the person, it [reason] is incorruptible, and if one only says to him in such a condition that it would be at least possible he will soon have to stand before a judge, then one may leave him over only to his own reflection, which will judge him in all probability according to the greatest severity.[145]

In this passage, Kant suggests that if one were to tell an agent on their deathbed that they soon might face an omniscient, omnipotent judge, this will suffice to induce sincerity in the agent's conscience (and, therefore, a suitable state of repentance and humility for past misdeeds). Once again, the training of conscience is second-personal, although in this passage Kant does not say that there is a positive duty to behave in this way toward those on their deathbeds.

In addition to training conscience in the wrong way, agents can fail to fulfill the duty to train conscience entirely. Kant thinks of this as a kind of negative training, training oneself to pay no heed to the voice of conscience, and he associates it with truly vicious agents. For example, in the "Miscarriage" Kant discusses the fact that happiness is not distributed in accordance with virtue. Kant says that someone writing a theodicy might deny this kind of counter-purposiveness; s/he might argue that, although it seems like the vicious are sometimes happy (and conversely), in reality immoral action already brings with it its own punishment insofar as "the inner reproofs of conscience plague profligates worse even than furies."[146] Kant, however, rejects this argument. He rejects it because it rests on the false assumption that the conscience of a vicious person will be like the conscience of a virtuous person. According to Kant, "the more virtuous the man is, the harder it [his conscience] will punish him on account of the slightest overstepping, which the moral law in him disapproves."[147] This is in contrast with what happens in the vicious:

> the small scoldings, however, which he [a vicious person] might make to himself now and then, he makes to himself either not at all through con-science, or, if he has thereof yet something in himself, then they [the scold-ings] are richly counterbalanced and compensated through the sensible enjoyments which he alone finds [to his] taste.[148]

---

[145] RGV, AA 06: 070.08–14. In this passage, Kant infers that reason is "incorruptible" from the fact that it speaks freely "about him, the person." This inference is initially puzzling given Kant's preoccupation with insincerity, especially (as seen in Section 2 of this work) as manifested in inner professions. Indeed, one might expect Kant to say that precisely because reason is free and making first-personal judgments, it not only is corruptible but also often is corrupted. I suggest that one way to make sense of this inference is along the lines of Kant's argument that because conscience involves judging the subject, its judgments are immediate and, therefore, immune to error.

[146] MpVT, AA 08: 261.03–04. [147] MpVT, AA 08: 261.07–09.

[148] MpVT, AA 08: 261.14–17.

Similarly, in the lecture notes it is asserted that the vicious have learned to ignore their consciences, in effect training their consciences negatively – habituation directly opposed to that which the moral law prescribes.[149] Traces of this view can be found in the *Groundwork*: in one of the examples Kant uses to illustrate the Categorical Imperative, Kant imagines an agent who desires to tell a lying promise in order to get some ready money but who "yet however has so much conscience to ask himself: is it not disallowed and contrary to duty" to do so.[150] It also is in keeping with Kant's idea (discussed in Section 2 of this Element) that conscienceless action should be understood as action that involves paying no heed to conscience rather than action on the part of an agent who literally has no conscience.

It is precisely because Kant thinks that the faculty of conscience can be trained and that it can be trained poorly or well that his claims about acting in accordance with conscience cannot be understood merely as: if an agent is not reproved by conscience, then s/he has done all that the moral law can demand of him/her. This conditional holds only if the agent has a healthy conscience and s/he has exercised it in that instance, neither of which is a trivial condition on Kant's account. From this it may be seen that moral training and habituation have an important role to play in Kant's ethical thought and that they manifest especially in his theory of conscience.

3.2 Nonaccidental Rightness

The centerpiece of Barbara Herman's now well-known discussion of Kant on moral worth is the so-called nonaccidental rightness condition (NRC). Herman's argument can be divided into two main steps. First, she maintains that, according to Kant, an action has moral worth if but only if it is done from the motive of duty: "Kant seems . . . quite clear about his conclusion: an act has moral worth if and only if it is done from the motive of duty."[151] Second, she explains why the motive of duty confers this special moral worth. It is in this second step of the argument that the NRC becomes important.

According to Herman, there is another biconditional that can be used to understand why the motive of duty confers this special value: an action has moral worth if and only if it is nonaccidentally right. Thus, to say that an action has moral worth, "we need to know that it was no accident that an agent acted as duty required," and so a motive is needed "that will *guarantee* that the right

---

[149] V-Mo/Mron II, AA 29: 623. However, there are also passages in the lecture notes that suggest the contrary: that even when wrong action is not punished externally, an agent's conscience metes out punishment (V-Phil-Th/Pölitz, AA 28: 1082).

[150] GMS, AA 04: 422.19–20.   [151] Herman (1993, 1).

action will be done."[152] Herman examines several different motives to see whether they will satisfy this condition. The profit motive, according to Herman, will not confer moral worth because it is unreliable: "When it leads to dutiful actions, it does so for circumstantial reasons."[153] Making a good profit generally might prescribe being honest with customers (and so duty and profit will align), but sometimes making a good profit will require an agent to perform an immoral action. Herman argues that the inclination to help others fails to confer moral worth for the same reason: "the class of actions that follows from the inclination to help others is not a subset of the class of right or dutiful actions."[154] Helping others generally seems good, but if I am acting solely on the inclination to help others, then I might wind up helping them to carry out nefarious plans. In fact, according to Herman, any nonmoral motive faces this problem. If an agent acts on a nonmoral motive, then, says Herman, it is merely a lucky accident that s/he acts in conformity with duty. Thus, nonmoral motives cannot confer moral worth:

> nonmoral motives may well lead to dutiful actions, and may do this with any degree of regularity desired. The problem is that the dutiful actions are the product of a fortuitous alignment of motives and circumstances.[155]

But the motive of duty, the moral motive, is not like this, at least according to Herman. The motive of duty leads nonaccidentally to action that is in conformity with duty:

> when we say that an action has moral worth, we mean to indicate that the agent acted dutifully from an interest in the rightness of his action: an interest that therefore makes its being a right action the nonaccidental effect of the agent's concern.[156]

> When an agent does act dutifully from the motive of duty, when his maxim of action has moral content, it is not a matter of luck that the *action* has moral worth.[157]

Herman's NRC emerges from this:

> NRC: An action that is from duty necessarily is in conformity with duty.

Herman does not explain why the motive of duty has this property. However, she does maintain that Kant subscribed to the NRC, and she also maintains that the NRC is independently philosophically plausible. Moreover, Herman seems to be in good company in believing this: according to Marcia Baron, Herman's NRC "is (among Kantians) uncontroversial."[158]

---

[152] Herman (1993, 9 and 3, emphasis mine).   [153] Herman (1993, 3).   [154] Herman (1993, 5).
[155] Herman (1993, 6).   [156] Herman (1993, 6).   [157] Herman (1993, 13).
[158] Baron (1995, 174). I owe this reference to Sverdlik (2001, 303).

Nonetheless, the NRC is wrong, and Kant's theory of conscience reveals why. As Section 2 of this Element demonstrated, throughout his writing, both published and unpublished (and, to judge from the notes examined earlier, in his lectures), Kant allowed for the possibility of errors in judgment regarding whether an action is a duty. But if this is conjoined with some plausible assumptions about the connections between cognitive and motivational states, it follows immediately that the NRC is false; an agent can act from duty but not in conformity with duty on Kant's account. Of course, some might not be bothered by this. They might say that this is so much the worse for Kant: they might say that they are more interested in setting out a plausible ethical theory than in setting out Kant's ethical theory, and if this philosophical project requires disagreeing with Kant in order to affirm the NRC, so be it. In my view, however, this would be misguided. It would be misguided not because exegetical and philosophical questions cannot be disentangled. On the contrary, I think it would be misguided because I think Kant was right about this: the NRC is not philosophically plausible. Agents do make mistakes about their duties, and it would be easy, I think, to come up with both tragic and comic (and tragicomic) examples from history of such agents acting out their errors. So what led Herman (and her followers) to ascribe the NRC to Kant?

Herman concentrates on part I of the *Groundwork*, and in a passage that is crucial for her purposes Kant says the following:

> I pass over here all actions which already are recognized as contrary to duty ... for with them there is indeed not even the question whether they might be occurring *from duty* since they even conflict with it.[159]

On the basis of this, it might be inferred that, according to Kant, if an action conflicts with duty, then it cannot be from duty. But an action conflicts with duty if but only if it is not in conformity with duty. So it follows that, if an action is from duty, then it necessarily is in conformity with duty. Thus, there seems to be direct textual evidence for ascribing the NRC to Kant: Kant as much as says in this passage that the class of actions that are from duty is a subset of the class of actions that are in conformity with duty.

However, this evidence goes nowhere toward fixing the philosophical challenge to the NRC. Moreover, as a reading of Kant it is equivocal. The problem is that the class of actions Kant is talking about here is not the class of contrary-to-duty-actions *simpliciter*. Rather, it is the class of contrary-to-duty-actions-that-are-recognized-as-such, and this leaves open the possibility that an agent might fail to recognize an immoral action to be contrary to duty and, thus, that in such

---

[159] GMS, AA 04: 397.11–14.

an instance an agent might perform a contrary-to-duty-action from the motive of duty. So this passage is consistent with the denial of the NRC.

An alternate defense of the NRC is offered by John Hardwig. Hardwig suggests doctrinal grounds for ascribing the NRC to Kant. I shall summarize his argument before explaining what I take to be its fatal flaw. According to Hardwig, Kant is committed to two claims about duties: (1) all duties are universal; and (2) all duties are autonomous. Hardwig argues that Kant's commitment to (1) follows from his universalization formulation of the Categorical Imperative, "act only according to that maxim through which you at the same time can will that it become a universal law."[160] Hardwig then argues that Kant's commitment to (2) follows from his autonomy formulation of the Categorical Imperative, "the idea of the will of every rational being as a universal law giving will."[161] But according to Hardwig, (1) entails that (3) all agents have the same duties, and (2) entails that (4) all agents are able to perform any duty from duty, and (3) and (4) can be conjointly true only if (5) there are no mistaken moral judgments, from which it in turn follows that (NRC) there can be no actions that are from duty but not in conformity with duty. Hardwig explains all of this in the following passage:

> This union of the principle of autonomy and the principle of universality lies at the very heart of Kant's ethics, and he cannot give up either without destroying the core of his theory. He cannot give up the principle of universality, for without it he cannot claim that moral principles are objective, valid for all rational beings. And he cannot give up the principle of autonomy, for even rational principles will not yield categorical obligation unless they are products of *the agent*'s will, unless they are his principles ... Kant therefore needs to maintain that moral principles and judgments are both autonomous and universally valid. But he can maintain that they are both, only by denying the possibility of mistaken moral judgment. This is the fundamental reason why Kant *must* claim that there is no such thing as an action from duty but not in accord with duty.[162]

The main problem with Hardwig's argument is in the move from (1) to (3). The universalization formulation of the Categorical Imperative does not state that agents ought to act only according to universal laws or according to maxims that are universal laws; rather, it states that agents ought to act only on maxims that they can will at the same time as universal laws. Thus it need not be true on Kant's account that all agents have the same duties.

Hardwig might object to this in two ways. First, he might object that an agent can will something at the same time as a universal law if but only if it can be

---

[160] GMS, AA 04: 421.07–08, emphasis omitted.
[161] GMS, AA 04: 431.16–18, emphasis omitted.   [162] Hardwig (1983, 288).

a universal law and, thus, the gap that I am trying to open up between (1) and (3) is illusory. Second, he might point out that Kant says repeatedly that all rational agents have the same duties, so even if this does not follow from the universalization formulation of the Categorical Imperative, it still is a central part of Kant's practical philosophy.

I would like to say three things in response to these objections. First, Kant is at pains to point out that not all agents have the same duties. In fact, Kant thinks that the concept of duty does not apply to some rational beings at all. For example, in the *Opus Postumum* Kant conceives of God as all-obliging but never obliged;[163] in the *Groundwork* Kant says that imperatives, obligations, and duties do not apply to a holy or divine will;[164] and in the *Critique of the Power of Judgment* Kant suggests that an agent who cannot bring him/herself to believe in God may give up the end of promoting a world in which all are supremely virtuous and in which happiness is enjoyed in proportion to virtue, an end that Kant thinks agents rationally can pursue only if they believe in God, this notwithstanding the fact that Kant thinks there is a duty to adopt this end.[165]

Second, there are doctrinal reasons for thinking that neither Kant nor a Kantian should say that all agents have the same duties. In particular, Kant is, as is well known, committed to the principle that ought implies can (OIC).[166] But different agents have different abilities, whence it follows immediately (from OIC) that different agents might have different obligations. For example, Superman might have a duty of rescue that does not apply to another agent who is unable to fly. More prosaically, the rich have duties of charity that do not apply to the poor.

Third, the biconditional that says that an agent can will something at the same time as a universal law if but only if it can be a universal law is false. This is not the place to set out a detailed interpretation of the universalization formulation of the Categorical Imperative. The point for now is merely that what agents are able rationally to will depends to some extent on their beliefs, and Kant was very much aware of that (perhaps most obviously in the argument, gestured to two paragraphs earlier, that agents ought to promote a world in which all are supremely virtuous and in which happiness is enjoyed in proportion to virtue: as noted in Section 2 of this Element, Kant thinks that agents rationally can adopt this project only if they believe in God, immortality, and transcendental freedom). It is but an application of this point to the universalization formulation of the Categorical Imperative to see that what agents are able to will at the

---

[163] OP, AA 27: 124.22–26.   [164] GMS, AA 04: 414.01–10.

[165] KU, AA 05: 450.31–451.07.

[166] I canvass the textual grounds for ascribing OIC to Kant in chapter 1 of Kahn (2019b). I discuss the doctrinal grounds in chapter 2.

same time as universal laws depends to some extent on their beliefs. Because agents might have different beliefs, it follows from this that their duties might differ.

Now Hardwig concedes that the universalization formulation of the Categorical Imperative might be understood as I am suggesting here, but he contends that the problem remains. Hardwig argues that the problem "is not completely eliminated unless the principle of universalizability is itself a universal principle ... in the sense of 'accepted by every moral agent.'"[167] The problem Hardwig is talking about is that if the universalization formulation of the Categorical Imperative is not universally accepted, then there is some agent who does not accept it; and if there is some agent who does not accept the universalization formulation, then, for that agent, the universalization formulation would be in conflict with the autonomy formulation. I would like to say three things about this.

First, to insist on the universality of the universalization formulation is a far cry from insisting on the universality of all duties. Importantly for currently purposes, the universality of the universalization formulation is consistent with errors in moral judgment and, therefore, with the denial of the NRC. Thus, both direct textual and indirect doctrinal support for the NRC collapse under fire.

Second, I think we need to distinguish between operational acceptance and abstract acceptance. To see what I mean, note that two people might agree that a given instance of harming is wrong, but they might say that it is wrong for different reasons, one on the basis of the Categorical Imperative, the other on the basis of religious ethics. This would be an instance of operational agreement but abstract disagreement. In the same way, an agent might not accept Kant's abstract formulation of the Categorical Imperative, either because the agent is unfamiliar with it or because s/he thinks Kant gets things wrong. But s/he might reason in accordance with this formulation all the same. This is relevant for current purposes because Hardwig's point about autonomy requires only operational acceptance, for if agents reason in accordance with the universalization formulation, then it is their (autonomous) standard.

Third and finally, there are both textual and philosophical grounds for thinking that some kinds of error, like operational rejection of the universalization formulation of the Categorical Imperative, cannot be inculpable or, in fact, coherent.[168] Textually there are places in the lecture notes explored in Section 2 of this Element, like the distinction between natural and positive obligation, that are especially relevant. Alternatively, one might appeal to the fact that, in

---

[167] Hardwig (1983, 289).

[168] Along the same lines, there might be some kinds of ignorance that Kant would say cannot be inculpable.

admitting errors of moral judgment in the *Metaphysics of Morals*, Kant says merely that agents *sometimes* can be in error. Philosophically one might try to imagine an agent who autonomously decides to act heteronomously. This is contradictory. Of course, the decision to shuffle off one's agency can be coherent and permissible. But that is not what is at issue here. The point is that one cannot autonomously act heteronomously according to Kant's definitions of these words.[169]

Regardless of these more theoretical issues, however, hopefully enough has been said to show not only why the NRC, for all its widespread acceptance, is mistaken, but also that Kant, on the basis of his theory of conscience, would have rejected it. That is, it is a key aspect of Kant's theory of conscience that agents sometimes make mistakes in their judgments about the objective deontic status of an action, whence it follows that action that is from duty but nonetheless not in conformity with duty is possible on his account.

3.3 Moral Luck

The modern moral luck debate is characterized as having two sides: the Kantian side, which denies moral luck, and the Aristotelian side, which affirms it. This is captured in the following quotation from Nafsika Athanassoulis:

> Briefly, there are two main responses to the possibility of moral luck: one is to deny the existence of moral luck and attempt to make morality immune to luck (Kant), the other is to accept moral luck as an unavoidable part of the human condition (Aristotle).[170]

It also is reflected in the *Stanford Encyclopedia of Philosophy* entry on moral luck, which opens with the assertion that "[t]he idea that morality is immune from luck finds inspiration in Kant" and then later goes on to claim that "those who accept the existence of some type of moral luck reject . . . the Kantian conception of morality."[171]

Kant is taken to be the enemy of moral luck in general, both by those who affirm moral luck and by those who reject it. But he is taken to be the especial enemy of two particular species of moral luck: luck regarding moral worth and luck regarding responsibility for the results of our actions (resultant luck). As evidence for this, consider the following two quotations, the first about moral worth, the second about resultant luck:

---

[169] Some care is needed here in order to distinguish different aspects or layers of an action and also issues with temporal indexing, but hopefully the point is clear enough for present purposes.

[170] Athanassoulis (2005, 180n57).   [171] Nelkin (2013, sections 1 and 4.2, respectively).

(1) Julia Driver: "the Kantian system is actually constructed so as to avoid the impact of moral luck on moral worth."[172]

(2) Daniel Statman: "immunity from this kind of luck [viz., resultant luck] was Kant's main object in his famous opening passages of the *Grundlegung*."[173]

I cannot undertake here to show that Kant affirms moral luck in general. But I would like to set the historical record straight insofar as Kant's theory of conscience evinces how poorly the modern moral luck debate has understood his practical philosophy. In particular, I maintain that Kant's theory of conscience shows that he embraces both luck regarding moral worth and resultant luck.

Enough was said concerning the NRC in the previous subsection, I think, to enable me to be brief regarding how moral luck penetrates Kantian judgments of moral worth. On Kant's account, an action has moral worth only if it is in conformity with duty. Herman secures this conformity with the conjunction of the NRC and the motive of duty. This, arguably, would eliminate luck (and is what underlies Driver's claim). But the NRC is nontrivial for agents who are mistaken in their moral judgments, a possibility that, as seen in Section 2 of this Element, Kant explicitly considers more than once in setting out his theory of conscience. Because such agents might act from duty but not in conformity with duty, the NRC is false and, more, there is room for luck in Kantian judgments of moral worth. That is, there is room for luck in Kant's account of moral worth because it can be a matter of luck that an agent has in/correct beliefs about what his/her duty is and, thus, it can be a matter of luck that an agent acts in conformity with duty.[174]

---

[172] Driver (2013, 156).   [173] Statman (1993, 13).

[174] In contemporary discussions, the idea that judgments of moral worth are immune to luck is frequently taken as intuitive bedrock. For example, according to Singh, all sides in the debate accept that "one cannot perform a morally worthy action by accidentally doing the right thing," and he uses this, first, to reject other accounts and, second, to construct his own: the Guise of Moral Reasons account (Singh, 2020, 1).

The central thesis of Singh's account is that "[a] right action has moral worth if and only if the agent performs it on the basis of sufficient moral reasons as such" (Singh, 2020, 14). The problem with Singh's account is that it fails on its own terms: an agent who has corrupt moral principles might, on occasion, accidentally perform a right action on the basis of sufficient moral reasons as such if these principles happen to pre/proscribe the right thing for the right reasons. To illustrate how this can happen, suppose that Kantian moral principles are right and that utilitarian moral principles are wrong. Both Kantian moral principles and utilitarian moral principles yield a duty of beneficence. So a convinced utilitarian might perform a morally right beneficent action on the grounds that (1) this action will promote another agent's happiness, and (2) promoting this agent's happiness is a morally right thing to do in this instance. In this case, the agent's action would satisfy Singh's Guise of Moral Reasons account, but the agent's action would not satisfy the nonaccidentality condition with which Singh began (viz., that an agent cannot perform a morally worthy action by accidentally doing the right thing).

Some might resist this conclusion. Building on the passage from part I of the *Groundwork* explored in the previous subsection, some might maintain that, on Kant's account, an action has moral worth if but only if it is recognized as in conformity with duty and performed from that recognition. Indeed, this might allow us to salvage the intuitions behind the NRC. Although the NRC is unsustainable in light of Kant's affirmation of mistaken judgments about the deontic status of actions, "recognition" is a success-term: if an action is recognized to be in conformity with duty, then it is so. So if an action is performed from the recognition that it is right, then it will be nonaccidentally right.

I do not want to challenge this proposal on exegetical or philosophical grounds.[175] But I do want to point out that this proposal does not avoid the impact of moral luck on moral worth: precisely because of the possibility for mistaken judgment, whether an agent recognizes an action to be in conformity with duty can be subject to luck. Thus, even if this proposal is accepted, moral luck penetrates into the Kantian account of moral luck, its entry secured by (i) the fact that an action must be in conformity with duty for it to have moral worth, and (ii) Kant's theory of conscience.[176]

Explaining Kant on resultant luck will not be as brief. I begin with the following excerpt from the general introduction to the *Metaphysics of Morals*:

Singh might object that I am being uncharitable. One way in which this objection might be filled in is by pushing on the nonaccidentality condition. That is, Singh might object that, although there is a sense in which the agent in my example only accidentally does the right thing, it is not the sense that he has in mind with the nonaccidentality condition. Another way in which this objection might be filled in is by pushing on the Guise of Moral Reasons account. That is, Singh might object that the agent in my example, by virtue of having wrong moral principles, does not act on the basis of "sufficient moral reasons as such." I would like to say two things in reply to this.

First, neither of these objections is open to Singh. It is not open to Singh to appeal to the nonaccidentality condition in the way suggested in the previous paragraph because he deploys a similar kind of example against one of his interlocutors (Singh, in press, 10–11). And it is not open to Singh to appeal to the Guise of Moral Reasons account in the way suggested in the previous paragraph because doing so would undermine what he says about Huck Finn (viz., that despite the latter's corrupt moral principles, he nonetheless recognizes and acts from "considerations of Jim's personhood in virtue of tacitly taking them to constitute sufficient moral reason to help him" [Singh, in press, 22]). Second, the real point of all of this is that Kant would reject the thesis that judgments of moral worth are immune to luck. Given the problems that cleaving to this thesis seems to create, perhaps we should follow his lead.

[175] Kerstein claims that, if someone believes him/herself to have two jointly unfulfillable duties, then s/he can act from duty while believing him/herself to be acting contrary to duty (Kerstein, 2002, 208n6). If this is correct and if moral dilemmas can be real, then some care might be needed in setting out the recognition version of the NRC. But I think Kerstein's claim is mistaken: in such a situation, the motive of duty would not suffice to determine a course of action.

[176] I would like to thank an anonymous referee for pressing me to clarify this.

The good or bad consequences of an owed action – in the same way the consequences of the omission of a meritorious [action] cannot be imputed to the subject (*modus imputationis tollens*).

The good consequences of a meritorious – in the same way the bad consequences of a wrongful action can be imputed to the subject (*modus imputationis ponens*).[177]

Kant makes six claims here: (1) the good consequences of owed action cannot be imputed; (2) the bad consequences of owed action cannot be imputed; (3) the good consequences of the omission of meritorious action cannot be imputed; (4) the bad consequences of meritorious action cannot be imputed; (5) the good consequences of meritorious action can be imputed; and (6) the bad consequences of wrongful action can be imputed.

It is (5) and (6) that are most relevant for current purposes, for these two claims are at the heart of Kant's account of resultant luck. Now, technically speaking, these two claims are consistent with the denial of resultant luck. For example, Kant might have supplemented them with the caveat that consequences can be imputed only if they are not a matter of luck (good or bad). But as a matter of fact, Kant articulates no such caveat. Moreover, both of the examples that he gives that illustrate these principles at work, and also his unpublished reflections on these issues, suggest that Kant not only knew what he was about but also explicitly affirmed a more inclusive account of resultant luck than many in the modern debate.

The first example that is relevant here is Kant's (in)famous murderer at the door case. In this case, a murderer comes to the door to ask for the whereabouts of his intended victim. The homeowner knows what the murderer is planning to do and also believes that the victim is hiding in the basement. Kant then asks whether it would be permissible, from philanthropic motives (namely, to save the life of the intended victim), to lie to the murderer. The reason this case is so well known is that Kant answers in the negative: he says that lying in this case is not permissible, and many take that to be so absurd as to constitute a reductio of Kantian ethics in particular and deontological ethics in general. Reimagining Kant's case as taking place in Nazi Germany or the antebellum South makes vivid why Kant's answer is taken to be so wrong; it would be permissible, perhaps obligatory, to lie to the Gestapo hunting a runaway Jew who is hiding in your basement or to the KKK members hunting a runaway slave who is seeking shelter in your house.

Kantians have resisted this reductio in various ways. Some argue that Kantian ethics does not have this absurd result; others argue, further, that the particularities of Kant's case have been misunderstood and that it does not generalize in this

---

[177] MS, AA 06: 228.04–10.

way.[178] But these issues are not relevant for current purposes. What is relevant, and what frequently goes unnoticed in discussions of this example, is Kant's affirmation of resultant luck in discussing what should be imputed to an agent who lies to the murderer at the door:

> if you however lied and said he is not at home, and he is also actually (although unbeknownst to you) gone out where then the murderer encounters him in going away and carries out his deed on him: then you can with right be prosecuted as the author of the death of this person . . .. Whoever thus lies, so well-intentioned he thereby also might have intended to be, must answer and repent for the consequences thereof even before a civil court, so unforeseen as they also always might be.[179]

In this passage Kant says that an agent should be held responsible for the bad consequences (the death of the victim) of a wrongful action (lying) even if another agent intercedes between the original wrongful action and the consequences being imputed and no matter how unforeseen the consequences might be. From this it may be seen that Kant embraced resultant luck: agents who perform impermissible actions can be held responsible for the unlucky consequences of their actions (and agents who perform meritorious actions can be held responsible for the lucky consequences of their actions).

Now it might be objected that Kant is talking here about legal responsibility (before a court) rather than ethical responsibility (before one's conscience), and so perhaps the principles of consequence imputation from the *Metaphysics of Morals*, a text that deals primarily with legal issues in its first half, are intended only to apply to juridical duties, not to ethical ones. This would be problematic for my claim that Kant affirms resultant luck because resultant luck is taken to be a specifically ethical phenomenon.

I would like to say four things in response to this objection. First, Kant says that the liar will have to answer and repent for the consequences of the lie *even* before a civil court; this suggests that the imputation will be not only legal but also ethical.[180] Second, the principles of consequence imputation from the *Metaphysics of Morals* that are instanced in this example are set out in the general introduction to the *Metaphysics of Morals*, indicating that they are intended to be logically prior to the division of the text into legal and ethical issues. Indeed, the assertion that these principles of consequence imputation are intended to apply only to the legal sphere cannot be right for the simple reason that Kant did not think that there are any meritorious actions within the legal sphere; on Kant's account, merit does not apply to juridical duties.

---

[178] Wood (2008, chapter 14).   [179] VRML, AA 08: 427.11–20.
[180] I owe this point to John O'Dea.

Third, in his unpublished notes Kant is even more explicit than in the murderer at the door case. For example, in a reflection dated to 1773–8 Kant writes that "the effectus of a formaliter evil action, e.g., a lie, cannot juridice be imputed (only interne)."[181] In this short note Kant says that the effect of a wrongful action like lying cannot be imputed juridically; the effect only can be imputed internally, by an agent's conscience, which means: only ethically. Thus, Kant, in this note, is explicitly committing himself to resultant luck in the ethical sphere.

Fourth and finally, there is Kant's second example of consequence imputation, an example that, unlike the murderer at the door, is, I think, quite clearly about ethical rather than legal imputation. In his discussion of lying in the second half of the *Metaphysics of Morals*, Kant imagines a servant who, at the behest of his master, tells a lie when someone comes to the door looking for him. As a result, the master is able to commit a serious crime. Kant then asks:

> On whom does the guilt here fall (according to ethical principles)? Certainly on the latter [the servant], who here infringes on a duty to himself through a lie; [a lie] whose consequences now will be imputed to him by his own conscience.[182]

Note that in this example, just as in the murderer at the door example, the agent has the consequences of another person's actions imputed to him. This does not mean that these consequences are not imputed to the other person. Rather, I think it means that they are imputed to both people, the master and the servant. But the fact that they are imputed to the servant at all shows (again) how far Kant goes in affirming resultant luck: he allows for the intercession of another agent between the initial action and the imputed consequences.

There are three things here that tell in favor of my claim that this is about ethical rather than legal imputation. First, the example is in the second half of the *Metaphysics of Morals*, the half that is about ethical duties rather than juridical ones. Second, in a parenthetical remark at the beginning of this quotation Kant says that he is talking about guilt in accordance with ethical (rather than legal) principles. Third and finally, Kant claims that the consequences of the servant's lie will be imputed by the servant's own conscience. But this is exactly what sets ethical imputation apart from legal imputation: ethical imputation, for Kant, is imputation in the court of conscience, the metaphorical court of law; legal imputation, for Kant, is imputation in the actual court of law. From this it may be seen that close attention to Kant's theory of conscience reveals that moral luck,

---

[181] Refl, AA 19: 169.03–04.   [182] MS, AA 06: 431.31–34.

even moral luck regarding moral worth and the imputation of consequences, is part of his ethical theory.

Those in the modern moral luck debate might respond that their characterization of Kant as the enemy of moral luck is nonetheless well grounded in his texts. More, they might argue that it is grounded in aspects of his practical philosophy that are more foundational to Kant's thought than his theory of conscience and, thus, they might argue that their characterization is truer to the spirit of Kantian ethics than mine. I think that the previous subsection shows this kind of response to be unsustainable as far as moral worth is concerned, and I would like to conclude this subsection by showing that the same is true as far as responsibility for consequences is concerned.

The quotation from Statman refers to the opening lines of the *Groundwork*. It is in these lines that Kant declares that a good will is the only thing that is good without limitation. He then explains that the goodness of a good will does not derive from its effects:

> The good will is not regarded as good through that which it effects or is aimed at, not through its suitability for the achievement of any of its preset ends, but rather alone through the willing, i.e. in itself and for itself . . .. If at the same time through a special disfavor of fate or through the scanty outfit of a stepmother-ly nature this will is lacking entirely in capacities to push through its purpose; if with its greatest striving nevertheless nothing would be achieved by it and only the good will . . . remain: so it nevertheless would shine forth for itself like a jewel, as something which has its complete worth in itself.[183]

This passage is frequently taken to be definitive of Kant's ethics, and friends and foes alike take it to entail that "because states of affairs are not possible bearers of value in Kantian ethics, what actually happens seems to be outside the purview of morality."[184] But if actual consequences do not matter, then (*a fortiori*) (un)lucky consequences do not matter. That seems to be what Statman has in mind.

However, I think this interpretation is mistaken. A good will might be the only unlimited good, and its goodness might be nonderivative and in itself. But that does not mean that there are no other things that are also good, nor does it mean that the conjunction of something that is of limited value with a good will cannot be better in some sense than a good will alone. Indeed, precisely this idea is crucial to Kant's highest good argument, one of the arguments explored in Section 2 of this Element. As seen earlier, Kant thinks that virtue by itself is the supreme good, but it is incomplete; for the complete good, happiness,

---

[183] GMS, AA 04: 394.13–26.   [184] Herman (1993, 95).

a conditioned good, must be conjoined to virtue. Along the same lines, a good will might shine forth like a jewel all by itself irrespective of its setting, and so an impartial rational spectator might take a good will to be good regardless of whether it attains its ends. But that is perfectly consistent with the idea that a beautiful jewel can be complemented with a matching setting, and so an impartial rational being might prize more highly a good will that attains its ends than one that is constantly floundering about.

Moreover, a close inspection of Kant's principles of consequence imputation reveal that they are precisely formulated so as to preserve the action-guiding nature of the Categorical Imperative: good consequences of vicious action are not to be imputed, so an agent would have no moral reason to perform a wrong action; bad consequences of a meritorious action are not to be imputed, so an agent would have no moral reason to omit a good action; and so on. Given how well these principles dovetail with Kant's ideas about the Categorical Imperative, and given that those in the moral luck debate seem to be basing their reading of Kant on an extrapolation from a few misunderstood lines of a popular work, one intended for more general readership than the texts explored in Section 2 of this Element, it seems to me that the origin of the moral luck debate might be a straw-man fallacy, one that can be uncovered only through a discussion of Kant's theory of conscience: it is conscience that, for Kant, is responsible for ethical (as opposed to legal) action and consequence imputation.

3.4 GOG

In this subsection I am going to discuss a thesis called the guise of the objectively good (GOG).[185] The GOG says that agents always represent their ends as objectively good. It is the cornerstone of Christine Korsgaard's famous regress argument, her interpretation of Kant's derivation of the humanity formulation of the Categorical Imperative. As such, she has put it forth as both exegetically and philosophically plausible in multiple works:

(1) In the argument for the Formula of Humanity, as I understand it, Kant uses the premise that when we act we take ourselves to be acting reasonably and so we suppose that our end is, in his sense, objectively good.[186]

(2) He [Kant] started from the fact that when we make a choice we must regard its object as good. His point is the one I have been making – that being human we must endorse our impulses before we can act on them.[187]

---

[185] Kahn (2013).   [186] Korsgaard (1996a, 116).   [187] Korsgaard (1996b, 122).

(3) ... as rational beings, who are conscious of our choices and the grounds of those choices, we can pursue our ends only if we are satisfied that doing so is good – that is, that our ends are worthy of pursuit.[188]

(4) ... when we act, we take our natural good to be an objective good.[189]

(5) If I am to will an end ... [t]hat amounts to thinking that it should appear as worthy of pursuit from any motivational point of view . . .. Call that being "absolutely" valuable.[190]

However, Korsgaard is not the only Kantian who advocates the GOG. It is also adopted by many other prominent Kantian ethicists:

(1) Allen Wood, talking about Kant's derivation of the humanity formulation of the Categorical Imperative, says the following: "Kant's argument is based on the idea that to set an end is to attribute objective goodness to it."[191]

(2) Henry Allison, talking about maxim adoption, asserts that "[r]ational agents can, of course, adopt foolish or immoral maxims, but they cannot adopt maxims without taking them to be, in some sense, justified (although this may very well rest on self-deception)."[192]

(3) Stephen Engstrom, talking about adopting an end, claims that "in taking something as the object of one's will (that is, in adopting it as an end), one claims it to be good."[193]

(4) Herman, in talking about maxims of action, says, "Maxims of action express what an agent wills: her action and intention as understood to be good and chosen because good."[194]

I think the easiest way to understand the GOG is by contrast with other alternative theses one might adopt. There are two. The first might be called the guise of the good (GG); it says that agents always represent their ends as good. The second might be called the negation of the guise of the good (NGG); it says that agents do not always represent their ends as good.

The GOG is considerably stronger than the GG: the GOG entails the GG, but the converse entailment does not hold. That is because regarding an end as good is not the same as regarding it as objectively good. An end is objectively good if but only if it is unconditionally good or it is conditionally good and the conditions of its goodness are satisfied. In other words, an end is objectively good if but only if it is *ultima facie* justified or all-things-considered good. So an end that is merely *prima facie* or merely some-things-considered good is not

---

[188] Korsgaard (2004, 93).   [189] Korsgaard (2011, 106).   [190] Korsgaard (2013, 11).
[191] Wood (1999, 129); he repeats this in Wood (2008, 91).   [192] Allison (1990, 91).
[193] Engstrom (1992, 760).   [194] Herman (1993, 217).

"good enough" for the GOG even though it is "good enough" for the GG. Joseph Raz, who subscribes to the GG, explains this difference in terms of reasons; he says that the GG, unlike the GOG, allows for the possibility that an agent might act "for what he took to be the lesser reason."[195]

Which alternative (the GOG, the GG, or the NGG) one subscribes to will determine the kinds of narratives one constructs about agents. For example, consider Milton's Satan or Ovid's Medea. The former famously declares, "Evil be thou my good"; the latter (perhaps less famously) claims to be consciously engaged in wrongful action. The proponent of the NGG would not have to say anything further about these agents; the narratives that these agents tell about themselves might be true. The proponent of the GOG or the GG, by way of contrast, would have to say more. For example, the proponent of the GOG or the GG might say that Satan's claim involves a *de re* use of "evil" and a *de dicto* use of "good," or s/he might say that Satan is merely embracing evil as a means to some end he regards as objectively good, like liberty, power, or glory. Thus, Satan's claim is rescued from (what the proponent of the GOG or the GG regards as) its surface-level incoherence by giving it a more complex interpretation, and something similar would be done for Medea.

Along the same lines, the story of Leontius can be used to illustrate the difference between the GG and the GOG. Leontius wants to look at some corpses, and he can be interpreted as regarding such an action as good insofar as it would afford him pleasure. Nonetheless, he regards looking at these corpses as shameful, something he ought not to do, not all-things-considered or objectively good. When he looks at the corpses anyway, a proponent of the GG might say that Leontius acts for what he regards as the lesser reason. But this explanation is not open to the proponent of the GOG. The proponent of the GOG would have to say something else, such as that Leontius regarded

---

[195] Raz (2008, 22n22). Hegel seems to use the GG as the basis for a critique of Fries. Hegel ascribes to Fries the view that an agent acts permissibly if but only if s/he performs an action s/he takes to be at least *prima facie* good, and Hegel then appeals to the GG to conclude that this view would render all actions permissible:

> everyone always wills something positive, and therefore, on the view we are considering, something good. In this abstract good the distinction between good and evil has vanished together with all concrete duties; for this reason, simply to will the good and to have a good intention in acting is evil rather than good, because the good willed is only this abstract form of good and the task of giving it determinacy thus falls to the arbitrary will of the subject. (Hegel, 2008, 143)

Although Hegel's attack on Fries seems to be based on a misinterpretation of the latter's views (and Hegel overlooks the fact that someone might reject the GG in favor of the NGG), Hegel is right in concluding, on the basis of the GG, that "to have a good intention in acting is evil rather than good" if by "to have a good intention" he means to act for the lesser good. For helpful discussion, see Wood (1990, chapter 10).

satisfying his necrophilic appetite as objectively good on the grounds that it is a harmless gratification that will enable him to avoid some more deleterious outbreak in the future (or the proponent of the GOG might say that Leontius was literally overcome by his desire and thus that "his" looking at the corpses was not an action at all).

What makes the Kantian commitment to the GOG distinctive is that Kantians are committed to bridge principles that make morality, reasons, goodness, and justification all go together. And it is precisely this that reveals why Kant is not committed to the GOG. As seen in the preceding subsections of this Element, Kant thinks that (1) an agent's conscience will represent his/her duty to him/her, (2) an agent can be mistaken about the deontic status of a given action, (3) an agent who acts in accordance with conscience has done all that (morally) can be demanded of him/her, and (4) vicious agents pay no heed to conscience. To see why this is inconsistent with the GOG, note that if the GOG is correct, then a vicious agent is not one who pays no heed to conscience but rather one who erroneously represents his/her ends as objectively good. Whereas Kant would allow for a conscientious error of this kind and would say that if the error is conscientious, then any moral assessment of the agent is unimpugned, the proponent of the GOG would maintain otherwise. Whereas Kant asserts that a vicious agent can perform an action notwithstanding the voice of conscience saying that it is not objectively good, the proponent of the GOG maintains that this is impossible. From this it may be seen that, although the GOG is quite popular among Kantians, it is at loggerheads with Kant's theory of conscience and, thus, with a central part of his practical philosophy.

3.5 Puzzles

I have argued for the following theses on the basis of Kant's theory of conscience: (1) Kant thinks that agents can make mistakes when judging the deontic status of an action; (2) Kant's commitments entail that an agent can act from duty but not in conformity with duty (thus the NRC should not be ascribed to Kant and neither should the denial of moral luck with regard to moral worth); and (3) Kant's commitments entail that an agent can pursue an end that s/he does not regard as objectively good (thus the GOG should not be ascribed to Kant). But the conjunction of these three theses opens up the doors for various puzzle cases, puzzle cases that are especially puzzling on account of Kant's insistence in both doctrine and example that the (potentially un/lucky) consequences of a meritorious or vicious action can be imputed to an agent, also a part of his theory of conscience (insofar as imputation occurs by means of an agent's conscience).

We already have seen how Kant handles two kinds of puzzle case. If an agent has acted in accordance with his/her (healthy) conscience, then, according to Kant, s/he has done all that morality can demand of him/her. Thus, if, following his/her fallible best judgment that a given action is permissible, an agent does something that is objectively wrong, s/he cannot be held accountable for performing a wrong action or, it seems, for the bad consequences of this wrong action. Conversely, if, following his/her fallible best judgment that a given action is impermissible, an agent does something that is objectively right, s/he is nonetheless to some extent to blame, and it is questionable whether Kant would hold the agent responsible for the good consequences of the action even if it is objectively meritorious (indeed, there are grounds for thinking that Kant would hold such an agent responsible for the bad consequences of his/her trying to act contrary to the moral law). This second kind of case, when an agent performs a right action while following his/her best judgment that what s/he is doing is wrong, has come to be known as inverse akrasia, and it is frequently illustrated using Mark Twain's portrayal of Huck Finn. The idea is that Huck Finn believed the racist moral framework prevalent at the time and takes his loyalty to Jim to be a weakness, and because of this Huck mistakenly takes his decision not to turn Jim over to the slave-catchers to be wrongful.

I do not intend here to engage with the question of how correctly to interpret Mark Twain's novel, nor do I intend here to pick up the literature on inverse akrasia more broadly. However, I do want to make three points about how Kant's theory of conscience can be used to shed light on all of this. First, Kant's position on inverse akrasia (agents acting permissibly despite acting contrary to their own best judgment about what they should do) and his position on what might be called inverse continence (agents acting impermissibly despite acting in accordance with their own best judgment about what they should do) are both taken from the same place: his theory of conscience. The modern debate, however, is more splintered. Moreover, in the modern debate philosophers focus on inverse akrasia and neglect inverse continence.

There are historical reasons for this neglect. The modern debate was seeded by an article on conscience that looks at agents who, like Huck Finn, have bad principles.[196] Nonetheless, it seems to me that this neglect should be rectified. Developing a position on inverse continence is, I think, vital to any plausible ethical theory. I also think that exploring what should be said about inverse continence can shed light on what should be said about inverse akrasia. Kant's position on inverse continence (that agents who act conscientiously have done

---

[196] Bennett (1974). It is worth noting that Kant is also guilty of this kind of neglect: although he gives general principles for the imputation of good consequences of meritorious actions, he only gives examples of imputation of the bad consequences of vicious actions.

all that can be demanded of them even if they act objectively wrongly) seems to me like a good starting point for rectifying this neglect even if, ultimately, this position ends up being superseded by a more nuanced one.

Second, the modern debate is carried out largely in terms of what an agent has most reason to do. Indeed, various philosophers have argued that in at least some cases inverse akratics have most reason to act akratically. But as I have tried to show in the previous subsections of this Element, the issues that give rise to the possibility of inverse akrasia (and inverse continence) intersect also with the moral luck debate and with questions about consequence imputation. Insofar as Kant developed positions on these issues (even if his positions have been largely misunderstood, ignored, or unexplored), I think that, again, they can serve as good starting points for examining these intersections even if, ultimately, Kant's positions end up being superseded by others.

Third and most importantly, Kant's discussion makes evident the fact that the joint phenomena of inverse akrasia and inverse continence can be borne out in two distinct ways. That is, an agent's mistaken judgment about the deontic status of an action can result from mistaken principles or from mistaken reasoning. For examples of mistaken reasoning, one might point to the manifold disagreements about the deontic status of various maxims on the basis of Kantian principles: more than 200 years after Kant's death, people are still debating about the implications of the various formulations of the Categorical Imperative. Clearly, mistakes in reasoning about these issues are possible. If an agent makes such a mistake, s/he might adopt a mistaken principle. S/he then might act conscientiously but wrongly, or s/he might end up adopting other mistaken principles on the basis of the first.

There are two reasons why this is important. First, it is unclear whether the same account should be given of inverse akrasia/continence that results from mistaken principles and of inverse akrasia/continence that results from mistaken reasoning. Kant does not distinguish between different kinds of mistaken judgment on the basis of the source of the error, and some might maintain that if, as suggested toward the end of the discussion of the NRC in subsection 3.2, all agents reason in accordance with the Categorical Imperative, then mistaken principles must result from mistaken reasoning, so the difference between these two is not a deep one. But Kant might not have thought much about this issue, and it is unclear whether the claim that all mistaken principles must result from mistaken reasoning is sustainable: plainly, more work remains to be done here.

The second reason why this is so important is that it reveals additional puzzle cases. For example, it is conceivable that an agent with mistaken principles could make a mistake in reasoning from these principles and that the two mistakes would "cancel out," so to speak, so that his/her judgment about the deontic status of an action is objectively correct even though s/he arrived at it in the wrong way. Of course, neither mistaken principles nor mistaken reasoning necessarily will result in a mistaken conclusion: the principle of utility, for example, sometimes will yield the right results, and mistaken reasoning sometimes is innocuous. But the combination of mistaken reasoning from mistaken principles to the right result seems like it warrants special treatment. A well-developed theory of conscience like Kant's, I suggest, is a good framework for such treatment to begin.

4 Conclusion

My goal in this work has been to give a brief but accessible exposition of Kant's theory of conscience. I began by examining Kant's various definitions of conscience and the functions that he ascribes to it. These functions include: determining whether an agent has acted according to his/her best judgment about what s/he ought to do; warning an agent if s/he is about to act wrongly; causing an agent to feel pain if s/he has acted wrongly; and determining whether an agent's best judgment about what s/he ought to do was negligent. I argued that, although Kant thinks that conscience cannot err, he does not think that agents never are mistaken in trying to determine what they ought to do. On the contrary, Kant is open about the possibility of such mistakes, and he uses his theory of conscience to provide a philosophical provision for them. According to Kant, if an agent has acted according to conscience, then nothing more can be demanded of him/her, and conversely.

However, Kant thinks that agents cannot be mistaken in their second-order judgments about whether they believe that a given action is im/permissible, and exactly this helped to elucidate Kant's position on freedom of conscience. I maintained that one reason for the amplification of Kant's views on conscience has to do with historical context, including the increased censorship and forced professions in the wake of the shift in power from Frederick the Great to Frederick William II. I argued that, for Kant, a forced profession involves both affiant and authority in a violation of conscience, at least if the profession in question cannot be known apodictically. I used this to draw out a point of contact between Kant's theory of conscience and his highest good argument, namely Kant's emphasis on the idea that the existence of God and the immortality of the soul have only subjective certainty (as such, to force someone to profess belief in them is to give scandal).

I then turned to philosophical issues in the treatment of Kantian ethics. I argued that Kant's theory of conscience reveals one way in which Kant thinks that proper moral education, habituation, and training are essential. I used

Kant's theory of conscience to explain why Kantians should not accept the nonaccidental rightness condition, and I also used it to show that the standard picture of Kant as the enemy of moral luck is grossly mistaken. In subsection 3.4, I argued that Kant's theory of conscience reveals that he was not committed to the guise of the objectively good thesis, and in subsection 3.5 I wrapped up with a discussion of various puzzle cases. My hope is that this work will inspire others, either to correct the errors they find here or to follow the various guiding threads I have tried to expose to greater depths.

References

Allison, Henry. 1990. *Kant's Theory of Freedom*. Cambridge University Press.

Athanassoulis, Nafsika. 2005. *Morality, Moral Luck and Responsibility*. Palgrave Macmillan.

Baron, Marcia. 1995. *Kantian Ethics Almost Without Apology*. Cornell University Press.

Beaver, David I. and Geurts, Bart. 2014. "Presupposition," *The Stanford Encyclopedia of Philosophy* (Winter Edition), Edward N. Zalta (ed.), URL = https://plato.stanford.edu/archives/win2014/entries/presupposition. Accessed 10.19.2020.

Bennett, Jonathan. 1974. "The Conscience of Huckleberry Finn." *Philosophy*, 49 (188): 123–134.

Driver, Julia. 2013. "Luck and Fortune in Moral Evaluation," in *Contrastivism in Philosophy* (ed. by Martijn Blaauw). Routledge: 154–172.

Engstrom, Stephen. 1992. "The Concept of the Highest Good in Kant's Moral Theory." *Philosophy and Phenomenological Research*, 52: 747–780.

Fichte, Johann Gottlieb. 2005. *The System of Ethics*. Translated and edited by Daniel Breazeale and Günter Zöller. Cambridge University Press.

Fries, Jakob Friedrich. 1818. *Handbuch der praktischen Philosophie*. Mohr und Winter.

Hardwig, John. 1983. "Action from Duty but Not in Accord with Duty." *Ethics*, 93 (2): 283–290.

Hegel, Georg Wilhelm Friedrich. 2008. *Outlines of the Philosophy of Right*. Translated by T. M. Knox. Revised, edited, and introduced by Stephen Houlgate. Oxford University Press.

Hegel, Georg Wilhelm Friedrich. 2018. *The Phenomenology of Spirit*. Translated and edited by Terry Pinkard. Cambridge University Press.

Herman, Barbara. 1993. *The Practice of Moral Judgment*. Harvard University Press.

Kahn, Samuel. 2013. "The Guise of the Objectively Good." *The Journal of Value Inquiry*, 47 (1–2): 87–99.

Kahn, Samuel. 2015. "Kant's Theory of Conscience," in *Rethinking Kant: Volume IV* (ed. Pablo Muchnik and Oliver Thorndike). Cambridge Scholars Publishing: 135–156.

Kahn, Samuel. 2018. "Kant's Post-1800 Disavowal of the Highest Good Argument for the Existence of God." *Kant Yearbook*, 10 (1): 63–83.

Kahn, Samuel. 2019a. "The Problem of the Kantian Line." *International Philosophical Quarterly*, 59 (2/234): 193–217. DOI: 10.5840/ipq2019311128

Kahn, Samuel. 2019b. *Kant, Ought Implies Can, the Principle of Alternate Possibilities, and Happiness.* Lexington Press.

Kazim, Emre. 2017. *Kant on Conscience.* Brill.

Kerstein, Samuel. 2002. *Kant's Search for the Supreme Principle of Morality.* Cambridge University Press.

Korsgaard, Christine. 1996a. *Creating the Kingdom of Ends.* Cambridge University Press.

Korsgaard, Christine. 1996b. *The Sources of Normativity.* Cambridge University Press.

Korsgaard, Christine. 2004. "Fellow Creatures." *Tanner Lectures on Human Values*, 24: 77–110.

Korsgaard, Christine. 2011. "Interacting with Animals," in *The Oxford Handbook of Animal Ethics* (ed. by Tom Beauchamp and R. G. Frey). Oxford University Press: 91–118.

Korsgaard, Christine. 2013. "Kantian Ethics, Animals, and the Law." *Oxford Journal of Legal Studies*, 33 (4): 629–648.

Nelkin, Dana K. 2013. "Moral Luck," *The Stanford Encyclopedia of Philosophy* (Winter Edition), Edward N. Zalta (ed.), URL = https://plato.stanford.edu/archives/win2013/entries/moral-luck.

Paton, H. J. 1979. "Conscience and Kant." *Kant Studien*, 70: 239–251.

Raz, Joseph. 2008. "On the Guise of the Good," University of Oxford Legal Research Paper Series, Paper No. 43/2008. Available at SSRN: https://ssrn.com/abstract=1099838 or http://dx.doi.org/10.2139/ssrn.1099838.

Singh, Keshav. 2020. "Moral Worth, Credit, and Non-Accidentality." In *Oxford Studies in Normative Ethics* Volume 10 (ed. by Mark Timmons), Oxford University Press: 156–181.

Statman, Daniel. 1993. "Introduction," in *Moral Luck* (ed. by Daniel Statman). State University of New York Press: 1-34.

Sverdlik, Steven. 2001. "Kant, Nonaccidentalness and the Availability of Moral Worth." *The Journal of Ethics*, 5 (4): 293–313.

Wood, Allen. 1990. *Hegel's Ethical Thought.* Cambridge University Press.

Wood, Allen. 1999. *Kant's Ethical Thought.* Cambridge University Press.

Wood, Allen. 2008. *Kantian Ethics.* Cambridge University Press

For my teachers

Cambridge Elements ⹀

The Philosophy of Immanuel Kant

Desmond Hogan

Princeton University

Desmond Hogan joined the philosophy department at Princeton in 2004. His interests include Kant, Leibniz and German rationalism, early modern philosophy, and questions about causation and freedom. Recent work includes 'Kant on Foreknowledge of Contingent Truths,' Res Philosophica 91 (1) (2014); 'Kant's Theory of Divine and Secondary Causation', in Brandon Look (ed.) Leibniz and Kant, Oxford University Press (forthcoming); 'Kant and the Character of Mathematical Inference', in Kant's Philosophy of Mathematics Vol. I, Carl Posy and Ofra Rechter (eds.), Cambridge University Press (2020).

Howard Williams

University of Cardiff

Howard Williams was appointed Honorary Distinguished Professor at the Department of Politics and International Relations, University of Cardiff in 2014. He is also Emeritus Professor in Political Theory at the Department of International Politics, Aberystwyth University, a member of the Coleg Cymraeg Cenedlaethol (Welsh-language national college) and a Fellow of the Learned Society of Wales. He is the author of *Marx* (1980); *Kant's Political Philosophy* (1983); *Concepts of Ideology* (1988); *International Relations in Political Theory* (1992); *Hegel, Heraclitus and Marx's Dialectic*; *International Relations and the Limits of Political Theory* (1996); *Kant's Critique of Hobbes: Sovereignty and Cosmopolitanism* (2003); and *Kant and the End of War* (2012) and is currently editor of the journal *Kantian Review*. He is writing a book on the Kantian Legacy in Political Philosophy for a new series edited by Paul Guyer.

Allen Wood

Indiana University

Allen Wood is Ward W. and Priscilla B. Woods Professor emeritus at Stanford University. He was a John S. Guggenheim Fellow at the Free University in Berlin, a national Endowment for the Humanities Fellow at the University of Bonn and Isaiah Berlin Visiting Professor at the University of Oxford. He is on the editorial board of eight philosophy journals, five book series and the Stanford Encyclopedia of Philosophy. Along with Paul Guyer, Professor Wood is co-editor of the Cambridge Edition of the Works of Immanuel Kant and translator of the Critique of Pure Reason. He is the author or editor of a number of other works, mainly on Kant, Hegel and Karl Marx. His most recently published books are Fichte's Ethical Thought, (Oxford University Press, 2016) and Kant and Religion (Cambridge University Press, 2020). Wood is a member of the American Academy of Arts and Sciences.

About the Series

This Cambridge Elements series provides an extensive overview of Kant's philosophy and its impact upon philosophy and philosophers. Distinguished Kant specialists provide an up to date summary of the results of current research in their fields and give their own take on what they believe are the most significant debates influencing research, drawing original conclusions.

Cambridge Elements ⁼

The Philosophy of Immanuel Kant

Printed in the United States
by Baker & Taylor Publisher Services